The Path Toward Spirituality

Sacred Duties and Practices of the Bahá'í Life

Shahin Vafai

Palabra Publications

Books in the Essential Teachings Training Program:

The Path Toward Spirituality:
   Sacred Duties and Practices of the Bahá'í Life

Raising The Call:
   The Individual and Effective Teaching

ISBN 1-890101-18-4
Copyright © 1996, 1998 by Shahin Vafai
All rights reserved.
Published December 1996
2nd edition published September 1998

Palabra Publications
3735 B Shares Place
Riviera Beach, Florida 33404
USA
1-561-845-1919
1-561-845-0126 (fax)
palabrapub@aol.com
http://www.palabrapublications.com

Contents

Introduction

". . . true life is not the life of the flesh but the life of the spirit."[1]
—Bahá'u'lláh

Attaining Happiness

How to attain happiness is a question that sooner or later is asked by every human being. All around us, we see people trying to discover answers to this question. Many are trying to find happiness through material objects: by acquiring a larger house, a nicer car, a bigger television, a faster computer, or a fatter bank account. Relationships, whether for love or for gratification of physical desires, are pursued for happiness. Losing weight and becoming more physically attractive are viewed by masses of people as keys to happiness. Millions are trying to achieve happiness by escaping from their problems through a regular and heavy dose of entertainment or sports. Some are even trying more desperate and dangerous solutions, such as turning to alcohol or drugs.

Increasing numbers of people are realizing, however, that these answers do not bring about true happiness. The happiness resulting from these activities is temporary; it may last a few hours, days, or even years, but it does not endure. More importantly, these solutions do not result in true happiness because they fail to fulfill the basic purpose of our existence. The purpose of our lives is not just to acquire material objects, to be entertained, or to satisfy our physical desires. Our lives have a much more noble, a much loftier purpose. According to the Bahá'í Teachings, our lives have a spiritual purpose.

We can realize what this purpose is by learning about our true nature. The Bahá'í Writings state that "there are two natures in man: the physical nature and the spiritual nature."[2] The physical nature turns to

3

"bestial degradation and carnal imperfections"; whereas, the spiritual nature tends towards "moral sublimity and intellectual perfection."[3] If man's physical nature "should overcome the heavenly and merciful, he is, then, the most degraded of animal beings; and if the divine and spiritual should triumph over the human and natural, he is, verily, an angel."[4]

Man's spiritual nature has its origin with God, Who chose to confer upon us "the unique distinction and capacity to know Him and to love Him."[5] "Upon the reality of man . . . He hath focused the radiance of all of His names and attributes, and made it a mirror of His own Self."[6] We are made "in the image of God,"[7] that is, we have been given the capacity to reflect the qualities and virtues of God. The purpose of life is for us to fulfill this capacity, to cleanse the mirror of our hearts so that the image of divine qualities may appear therein: "every man imbued with divine qualities, who reflects heavenly moralities and perfections, who is the expression of ideal and praiseworthy attributes, is, verily, in the image and likeness of God."[8] Thus, "the ultimate aim in life of every soul should be to attain spiritual excellence. . . ."[9] By striving to attain spiritual excellence, we will achieve happiness. "The physical happiness of material conditions was allotted to the animal. . . . But the honor of the human kingdom is the attainment of spiritual happiness in the human world, the acquisition of the knowledge and love of God. The honor allotted to man is the acquisition of the supreme virtues of the human world. This is his real happiness and felicity."[10]

The key, therefore, to answering the question of how to attain happiness is learning how to develop our spiritual nature. This question has been answered by Bahá'u'lláh. He has taught that we can develop spiritually by fulfilling the twin, inseparable duties of recognizing the Manifestation of God and observing His ordinances. All those who have accepted Bahá'u'lláh as the Manifestation of God for this age strive to observe the ordinances He has set forth. His Teachings reveal that spiritual excellence is not an idealistic or impractical goal that only a few will reach. Rather, it is available to every person who makes the effort to understand and fulfill life's purpose by performing certain sacred duties and practices. The purpose of the present book is to discuss the basic features of these duties and practices, which are "the essential requisites for our spiritual growth" and which "represent the path towards the attainment of true spirituality."[11]

Duties and Practices of the Bahá'í Life and Principles of Spiritual Growth

Among the sacred duties ordained by Bahá'u'lláh are the practices of prayer, recital of the holy verses, meditation, study of the Faith, teaching, observance of divine laws and principles, material offerings, and service. These practices are not a believer's only obligations. They are, however, among the most fundamental, and they allow us to discover the many other aspects of the spiritual life.

As we learn about and carry out the spiritual practices of the Bahá'í life, it is important to keep in mind a number of principles. One principle is that of individual responsibility and initiative. It is noteworthy how private and personal most of the spiritual duties are. Bahá'u'lláh has placed the responsibility for spiritual growth on the shoulders of the individual believer: "For the faith of no man can be conditioned by any one except himself."[12] Each one of us "is responsible for one life only, and that is our own."[13] Because we are individually responsible for carrying out our spiritual practices, we cannot wait for others to remind us of our duties or to do the work for us. Nor can we become preoccupied with the efforts of others. We must take the initiative to educate ourselves about these practices and arise to fulfill them.

Another relevant principle is consistency. Spiritual practices are the food of the spirit; they nourish our souls. Just as we must feed our physical bodies every day, so must we regularly feed our spirits. We would consider it absurd to limit our bodies to one meal per week; how much more absurd must it be to let our spirits starve for long periods of time. If we keep in mind that the life of our spirit depends upon the regular and daily exercise of certain spiritual practices, then the challenges of the lack of time and energy become manageable. No matter how busy we may be, we still *make* time to eat. So should it be with our spiritual meals. Rather than thinking, "How can I do these things when I don't have any time in my life?", we will come to ask, "How can I manage my affairs to make time for my spiritual responsibilities?"

Spiritual development involves tests and difficulties, falling short and making new advances. Bahá'u'lláh says, "If adversity befall thee not in My path, how canst thou walk in the ways of them that are content with My pleasure? If trials afflict thee not in thy longing to meet Me, how wilt thou attain the light in thy love for My beauty?"[14] A test,

5

though it causes pain and suffering, is really a blessing in disguise because it allows us to refine our characters and to acquire spiritual qualities. "Men who suffer not, attain no perfection. The plant most pruned by the gardeners is that one which, when the summer comes, will have the most beautiful blossoms and the most abundant fruit."[15] We do not automatically overcome tests and difficulties. They can be either stumbling-blocks or stepping-stones. Effort on our part is required. We have been promised that we will never be tested beyond our capacity. Through patience and faithful obedience to the laws of Bahá'u'lláh, we can successfully pass all tests.

As we are struggling, we must remember that spiritual growth is a gradual process, not a one-time achievement. We should not expect to suddenly become transformed into spiritual beings. Our goal must be to steadily improve, little by little, day by day. We can encourage steady growth through regular review of our conduct and character by bringing ourselves "to account each day."[16] Bahá'u'lláh has written, "Let each morn be better than its eve and each morrow richer than its yesterday."[17]

One of the most important principles to consider is that spiritual development must lead to action. The sacred practices of prayer, meditation, and study attract to us spiritual energies. These energies must then be converted by the believer into action. For example, the Bahá'í Writings state, "Prayer and meditation are very important factors in deepening the spiritual life of the individual, but with them must go also action and example, as these are the tangible results of the former. Both are essential."[18] It is not enough to simply fill a car with fuel. This fuel serves no purpose unless the engine is started and the car begins to move. In the same way, we must use the spiritual fuel generated by the devotional exercises of the Bahá'í life to arise and to act. Action takes the form of service, teaching the Faith, and exemplifying divine qualities.

The Covenant of Bahá'u'lláh

The vehicle for the practical fulfillment of our spiritual duties is the Covenant of Bahá'u'lláh. It is "the potent instrument by which individual belief in Him is translated into constructive deeds."[19] The Covenant comprises divine arrangements to preserve the unity of the Faith.[20] Bahá'u'lláh, in the Book of the Covenant, confirmed the appointment of His son 'Abdu'l-Bahá as the interpreter of His Word and the Center of the Covenant.[21]

'Abdu'l-Bahá perpetuated the Covenant by establishing the Administrative Order.[22] He appointed Shoghi Effendi as the Guardian of the Faith and confirmed the guarantee of divine guidance for the institution of the Universal House of Justice, which Bahá'u'lláh had described in His lifetime. The Guardianship and the Universal House of Justice can be seen as the "Twin Successors"[23] of Bahá'u'lláh and 'Abdu'l-Bahá. Their writings are authoritative statements of guidance for Bahá'ís. Today, the Universal House of Justice is the head of the Faith.

The Covenant has allowed the Bahá'í Faith to maintain its unity and integrity. This, in turn, has allowed individual Bahá'ís to know about and to fulfill God's purpose in this day. In addition, through the Covenant, "the meaning of the Word, both in theory and practice, is made evident in the life and work of 'Abdu'l-Bahá. . . ."[24] Bahá'u'lláh vested in 'Abdu'l-Bahá "the virtues of perfection in personal and social behavior,"[25] that humanity may have a model to follow. Because 'Abdu'l-Bahá embodied every Bahá'í ideal and incarnated every Bahá'í virtue,[26] Bahá'ís look to His example in striving to conform their inner lives to the ideal set by Bahá'u'lláh. The Universal House of Justice has explained that in thinking about 'Abdu'l-Bahá's divine example, "we may well reflect that His life and deeds were not acted to a pattern of expediency, but were the inevitable and spontaneous expression of His inner self. We, likewise, shall act according to His example only as our inward spirits, growing and maturing through the disciplines of prayer and practice of the Teachings, become the wellsprings of all our attitudes and actions."[27]

Thus, the sacred duties and practices of the Bahá'í life are the means by which we can make progress on the spiritual path and, thereby, fulfill the purpose of our lives. All who regularly and wholeheartedly carry out these practices will attain true and abiding happiness.

Quotations for Reflection

1. What is the present condition of mankind? What is the chief reason for the evils now rampant in society?

"Mankind is submerged in the sea of materialism and occupied with the affairs of this world. They have no thought beyond earthly possessions and manifest no desire save the passions of this fleeting, mortal existence. Their utmost purpose is the attainment of material livelihood, physical comforts and worldly enjoyments such as constitute the happiness of the animal world rather than the world of man."

('Abdu'l-Bahá, *The Promulgation of Universal Peace*, p. 335)

"Indeed, the chief reason for the evils now rampant in society is the lack of spirituality. The materialistic civilization of our age has so much absorbed the energy and interest of mankind that people in general do no longer feel the necessity of raising themselves above the forces and conditions of their daily material existence. There is not sufficient demand for things that we should call spiritual to differentiate them from the needs and requirements of our physical existence.

"The universal crisis affecting mankind is, therefore, essentially spiritual in its causes. The spirit of the age, taken on the whole, is irreligious. Man's outlook on life is too crude and materialistic to enable him to elevate himself into the higher realms of the spirit."

(On behalf of Shoghi Effendi, *Spiritual Foundations* #40)

2. What is the source of man's honor and happiness?

"The honor of man is through the attainment of the knowledge of God; his happiness is from the love of God; his joy is in the glad tidings of God; his greatness is dependent upon his servitude to God. The highest development of man is his entrance into the divine Kingdom, and the outcome of this human existence is the nucleus and essence of eternal life. If man is bereft of the divine bestowals and if his enjoyment and happiness are restricted to his material inclinations, what distinction or difference is there between the animal and himself? In fact, the animal's happiness is greater, for its wants are fewer and its means of livelihood easier to acquire. Although it is necessary for man to strive for material needs and comforts, his real need is the acquisition of the bounties of

God. If he is bereft of divine bounties, spiritual susceptibilities and heavenly glad tidings, the life of man in this world has not yielded any worthy fruit. While possessing physical life, he should lay hold of the life spiritual, and together with bodily comforts and happiness, he should enjoy divine pleasures and content. Then is man worthy of the title man; then will he be after the image and likeness of God, for the image of the Merciful consists of the attributes of the heavenly Kingdom. If no fruits of the Kingdom appear in the garden of his soul, man is not in the image and likeness of God, but if those fruits are forthcoming, he becomes the recipient of ideal bestowals and is enkindled with the fire of the love of God."

('Abdu'l-Bahá, *The Promulgation of Universal Peace*, p. 335)

3. Is it sufficient for a believer merely to accept and observe the teachings?

"It is not sufficient for a believer merely to accept and observe the teachings. He should, in addition, cultivate the sense of spirituality which he can acquire chiefly by means of prayer. The Bahá'í Faith, like all other Divine Religions, is thus fundamentally mystic in character. Its chief goal is the development of the individual and society, through the acquisition of spiritual virtues and powers. It is the soul of man which has first to be fed. And this spiritual nourishment prayer can best provide. Laws and institutions, as viewed by Bahá'u'lláh, can become really effective only when our inner spiritual life has been perfected and transformed. Otherwise religion will degenerate into a mere organization, and becomes a dead thing."

(On behalf of Shoghi Effendi, *Spiritual Foundations* #40)

4. What are the essential requisites for our spiritual growth? What represent the path towards the attainment of true spirituality?

"Bahá'u'lláh has stated quite clearly in His Writings the essential requisites for our spiritual growth, and these are stressed again and again by 'Abdu'l-Bahá in His talks and Tablets. One can summarize them briefly in this way:
"1.The recital each day of one of the Obligatory Prayers with pure-hearted devotion.

9

2. The regular reading of the Sacred Scriptures, specifically at least each morning and evening, with reverence, attention and thought.

3. Prayerful meditation on the Teachings, so that we may understand them more deeply, fulfil them more faithfully, and convey them more accurately to others.

4. Striving every day to bring our behavior more into accordance with the high standards that are set forth in the Teachings.

5. Teaching the Cause of God.

6. Selfless service in the work of the Cause and in the carrying on of our trade or profession.

"These points . . . represent the path towards the attainment of true spirituality that has been laid down by the Manifestation of God for this age."

(On behalf of the Universal House of Justice, *Lights of Guidance*, pp. 540-41)

5. The gifts of the spirit are received through what means?

"When a person becomes a Bahá'í, actually what takes place is that the seed of the spirit starts to grow in the human soul. This seed must be watered by the outpourings of the Holy Spirit. These gifts of the spirit are received through prayer, meditation, study of the Holy Utterances and service to the Cause of God. . . . [T]he evolution of the spirit takes place through ploughing up the soil of the heart so that it is a constant reflection of the Holy Spirit. In this way the human spirit grows and develops by leaps and bounds.

"Naturally there will be periods of distress and difficulty, and even severe tests; but if that person turns firmly towards the divine Manifestation, studies carefully His spiritual teachings and receives the blessings of the Holy Spirit, he will find that in reality these tests and difficulties have been the gifts of God to enable him to grow and develop."

(On behalf of Shoghi Effendi, *Living the Life*, pp. 35-36)

6. What is the significance of the Covenant?

". . . the power of the Covenant will protect the Cause of Bahá'u'lláh from the doubts of the people of error. It is the fortified fortress of the Cause of God and the firm pillar of the religion of God. Today no power can conserve the oneness of the Bahá'í world save the Covenant of God; otherwise differences like unto a most great tempest will encompass the Bahá'í world. It is evident that the axis of the oneness of the world of humanity is the power of the Covenant and nothing else.... Therefore, in the beginning the believers must make their steps firm in the Covenant so that the confirmations of Bahá'u'lláh may encircle them from all sides, the cohorts of the Supreme Concourse may become their supporters and helpers, and the exhortations and advices of 'Abdu'l-Bahá, like unto the pictures engraved on stone, may remain permanent and ineffaceable in the tablets of all hearts."

('Abdu'l-Bahá, *Tablets of the Divine Plan*, pp. 51-52)

Illustration

"A 'Mrs C' was an early believer who went to 'Akká. She belonged to a wealthy and fashionable group of people in New York. Her life had been conventional and rather unsatisfying. She had been a sincere Christian, but somehow had not gained much comfort from her religion. She had become somewhat melancholy. While traveling abroad, she had learned about 'Abdu'l-Bahá. She eagerly grasped His message and headed to the prison-city. Having arrived, she was fascinated by everything, most especially by the Master. She noticed that 'Abdu'l-Bahá always greeted her with 'Be happy!' The other members of the party were not addressed in the same way by Him. This troubled her. Finally she asked someone to ask the Master why He addressed her in this way. With 'His peculiarly illuminating smile', He replied, 'I tell you to be happy because we can not know the spiritual life unless we are happy!'

"Then Mrs C's dismay was complete, and her diffidence vanished with the fullness of her despair.

"'But tell me, what is the spiritual life?' she cried, 'I have heard ever since I was born about the spiritual life, and no one could ever explain to me what it is!'

"'Abdu'l-Bahá looked at His questioner again with that wonderful smile of His, and said gently: 'Characterize thyself with the characteristics of God, and thou shalt know the spiritual life!'—Few words, but they were sufficient. Mrs C began to wonder what 'Abdu'l-Bahá meant. The characteristics of God? They must be such attributes as love and beauty, justice and generosity.

"All day long her mind was flooded with the divine puzzle, and all day long she was happy. She did not give a thought to her duties, and yet when she arrived at the moment of her evening's reckoning, she could not remember that she left them undone.

"At last she began to understand. If she was absorbed in Heavenly ideals, they would translate themselves into deeds necessarily, and her days and nights would be full of light. From that moment she never quite forgot the divine admonition that had been granted her: 'Characterize thyself with the characteristics of God!'

"And she learned to know the spiritual life."

(*Vignettes from the Life of 'Abdu'l-Bahá*, pp. 116-17)

Study References

1. For more generally on the Bahá'í life, see the compilation *Living the Life*.

2. For more on the sacred duties of the Bahá'í life, see the *Kitáb-i-Aqdas* and the compilation *Spiritual Foundations: Prayer, Meditation, and the Devotional Attitude*.

3. The compilation *Bahá'u'lláh's Teachings on Spiritual Reality* contains a number of quotations on themes related to the spiritual life.

4. For more on the Covenant, see the compilation entitled *The Covenant* and the book *The Covenant: Its Meaning and Origin and Our Attitude Toward It*.

Prayer

"O Son of Light! Forget all save Me and commune with My spirit."[28]
—Bahá'u'lláh

The Bahá'í Writings declare that prayer is "absolutely indispensable" to "inner spiritual development."[29] "It is not sufficient for a believer merely to accept and observe the teachings. He should, in addition, cultivate the sense of spirituality which he can acquire chiefly by means of prayer."[30] The Faith has "the spiritual power to recreate us if we make the effort to let that power influence us, and the greatest help in this respect is prayer."[31]

What is prayer? Prayer is "conversation with God."[32] It is a state of spiritual communion between the worshiper and his Creator. If two people love one another, their greatest desire is to be in the presence of the other, to converse with their beloved. Similarly, the lovers of God desire to be in God's presence, to converse with Him. We can fulfill this desire through the practice of prayer. There are two types of prayers in the Bahá'í Faith, the obligatory prayer and other prayers, which are not obligatory.

Obligatory Prayer

Bahá'u'lláh, in the *Kitáb-i-Aqdas* (the Most Holy Book), ordains the recital of obligatory prayer: "We have commanded you to pray and fast from the beginning of maturity; this is ordained by God, your Lord and the Lord of your forefathers."[33] He further states, "In truth, I say that obligatory prayer and fasting occupy an exalted station in the sight

13

of God."[34] 'Abdu'l-Bahá has written that obligatory prayers are "conducive to humility and submissiveness, to setting one's face toward God and expressing devotion to Him."[35] Through the prayer, "man holdeth communion with God, seeketh to draw near unto Him, converseth with the true Beloved of one's heart, and attaineth spiritual stations."[36]

The obligatory prayer, as its name indicates, is mandatory. Bahá'u'lláh has revealed three Obligatory Prayers: the short, the medium, and the long. Bahá'ís are required to recite *one* of these Obligatory Prayers each day, but whichever one is selected must be said according to the specific instructions provided for that prayer. We are certainly free to offer more than one Obligatory Prayer if we wish, but we are not required to do so.

The short Obligatory Prayer is to be recited once a day at "noon."[37] "Noon" has been defined in the Writings as any time between noon and sunset.[38] If, on the other hand, a Bahá'í chooses to recite the medium Obligatory Prayer, then he must recite this prayer in the "morning, at noon, and in the evening."[39] "Morning" is the period from sunrise until noon; "noon" is from noon till sunset; and "evening" is from sunset till two hours after sunset.[40] The long Obligatory Prayer may be recited at any time during a twenty-four hour period. Like the short Obligatory Prayer, it is recited only once in the day.[41]

There are certain features and instructions that relate to all three Obligatory Prayers. The first is the direction in which the believer must face while praying. When reciting the obligatory prayer, the worshiper must face in the direction of the Shrine of Bahá'u'lláh, which is located near 'Akká, Israel. Like other regulations connected with the obligatory prayer, the act of turning towards the Shrine of Bahá'u'lláh is symbolic: "This is a physical symbol of an inner reality, just as the plant stretches out to the sunlight—from which it receives life and growth—so we turn our hearts to the Manifestation of God, Bahá'u'lláh, when we pray. . . ."[42]

At what age is the obligatory prayer binding? It is binding on believers beginning from the time of maturity, which Bahá'u'lláh has defined as 15 years of age.[43] One must recite the obligatory prayer until the age of 70, after which one is exempt.[44] Moreover, illness is an exemption: "In time of ill-health it is not permissible to observe these obligations. . . ."[45] Also, "Exemption from obligatory prayer is granted to those who find themselves in such a condition of insecurity that the saying of the Obligatory Prayers is not possible."[46] It should be noted that recital of the obligatory prayer is *not* suspended during travel, so long as one can find a "safe place"[47] to perform it.

Another feature is that the obligatory prayer is to be offered individually, "in the privacy of one's chamber,"[48] and not in congregation.[49] "Congregational prayer, in the sense of formal obligatory prayer which is to be recited in accordance with a prescribed ritual"[50] is not practiced in the Bahá'í Faith. The only exception to this law is the Prayer for the Dead, which is "recited by one of those present while the remainder of the party stands in silence."[51]

Ablutions precede the recital of obligatory prayer. Ablutions "consist of washing the hands and the face in preparation for prayer. In the case of the medium Obligatory Prayer, this is accompanied by the recitation of certain verses."[52] "That ablutions have a significance beyond washing may be seen from the fact that even should one have bathed oneself immediately before reciting the Obligatory Prayer, it would still be necessary to perform ablutions."[53]

There are certain bodily movements associated with the medium and long Obligatory Prayers.[†] These include raising one's hands in supplication, kneeling and bowing one's forehead to the ground, and other movements. Shoghi Effendi has explained that the few simple directions given by Bahá'u'lláh for the Obligatory Prayers are of a great spiritual help to the believer. Additionally, they help the worshipper "to fully concentrate when praying and meditating."[54] The short Obligatory Prayer does not involve any bodily movements; it only requires that the believer stand while praying.

The Bahá'í Writings indicate that the Obligatory Prayers have been endowed with a special potency, which only those who regularly recite them can adequately appreciate. "The friends should therefore endeavor to make daily use of these prayers, whatever the peculiar circumstances and conditions of their life."[55] We have been promised that "regular, wholehearted, obedience to this law will in itself nourish the growth of spirituality."[56]

[†]Some of the features and movements of the Obligatory Prayers are explained in Appendix A.

Other Prayers

We have, in addition to the Obligatory Prayers, many other beautiful and powerful prayers revealed by Bahá'u'lláh, the Báb, and 'Abdu'l-Bahá. They have revealed prayers for healing, unity, children, families, assistance, meetings, overcoming difficulties, and for many other purposes and occasions. Unlike the obligatory prayer, the non-obligatory prayers have no specific regulations. They may be recited at any time by anyone. There is no need to face the Shrine of Bahá'u'lláh or conform to the other requirements of the obligatory prayer. We are free to use these prayers in meetings, or individually, as we please.[57]

The Writings do, however, give us guidance on how we may generally improve the quality of our devotions. For example, whom should we turn to during prayer? We are free to pray either to God or His Manifestation, but the Writings state that "While praying it would be better to turn one's thoughts to the Manifestation as He continues, in the other world, to be our means of contact with the Almighty."[58] Further, "our prayers would certainly be more effective and illuminating if they are addressed to Him [God] through His Manifestation, Bahá'u'lláh."[59] Rather than focussing on the Manifestation's physical image, we should, while praying, try to think of His qualities and His Spirit.[60]

For what should we pray? "The true worshiper, while praying, should endeavor not so much to ask God to fulfill his wishes and desires, but rather to adjust these and make them conform to the Divine Will. Only through such an attitude can one derive that feeling of inner peace and contentment which the power of prayer alone can confer."[61]

Is it permissible to pray in our own words? The Writings state that "Of course prayer can be purely spontaneous. . . ."[62] We should, however, keep in mind that the prayers revealed by Bahá'u'lláh, the Báb, and 'Abdu'l-Bahá have a special power that human words lack: "the revealed Word is endowed with a power of its own. . . ."[63] In addressing God, Bahá'u'lláh has declared, "No words that any one beside Thee may utter can ever beseem Thee, and no man's description except Thine own description can befit Thy nature."[64]

Does God answer all prayers? 'Abdu'l-Bahá has said that God "answers the prayers of all His servants when according to His supreme wisdom it is necessary."[65] If we ask for things which God does not desire for us, there is no answer to our prayer. He explains, "We pray, 'O God! Make me wealthy!' If this prayer were universally answered, human affairs would be at a standstill. There would be none left to work in the streets, none to till the soil, none to build, none to run the trains. . . . The affairs of the world would be interfered with, energies crippled and progress hindered. But whatever we ask for which is in accord with divine wisdom, God will answer. Assuredly!"[66]

If God does answer our prayers, how do we know what the answer is? The Writings state that prayers are answered through action: "It is not sufficient to pray diligently for guidance, but this prayer must be followed by meditation as to the best methods of action and then action itself. Even if the action should not immediately produce results, or perhaps not be entirely correct, that does not make so much difference, because prayers can only be answered through action and if someone's action is wrong, God can use that method of showing the pathway which is right."[67] This quotation implies that we should pray about a question, meditate as to the best approach, and then act. Guidance is when the doors open after we have knocked.

Quotations for Reflection

1. What is the wisdom of prayer?

"The wisdom of prayer is this: That it causeth a connection between the servant and the True One, because in that state man with all heart and soul turneth his face towards His Highness the Almighty, seeking His association and desiring His love and compassion. The greatest happiness for a lover is to converse with his beloved, and the greatest gift for a seeker is to become familiar with the object of his longing; that is why with every soul who is attracted to the Kingdom of God, his greatest hope is to find an opportunity to entreat and supplicate before his Beloved, appeal for His mercy and grace and be immersed in the ocean of His utterance, goodness and generosity.

"Besides all this, prayer and fasting is the cause of awakening and mindfulness and conducive to protection and preservation from tests...."

('Abdu'l-Bahá, *Bahá'í World Faith*, p. 368)

17

2. What is the most acceptable prayer? Does prayer need to be prolonged?

"The most acceptable prayer is the one offered with the utmost spirituality and radiance; its prolongation hath not been and is not beloved by God. The more detached and the purer the prayer, the more acceptable is it in the presence of God."

(Selections from the Writings of the Báb, p. 78)

"We don't have to pray and meditate for hours in order to be spiritual." (On behalf of Shoghi Effendi, *Spiritual Foundations* #56)

3. What is the reason why privacy hath been enjoined in moments of devotion?

"The reason why privacy hath been enjoined in moments of devotion is this, that thou mayest give thy best attention to the remembrance of God, that thy heart may at all times be animated with His Spirit, and not be shut out as by a veil from thy Best Beloved. Let not thy tongue pay lip service in praise of God while thy heart be not attuned to the exalted Summit of Glory, and the Focal Point of communion." *(Selections from the Writings of the Báb, pp. 93-94)*

4. Do the obligatory prayers have a greater effectiveness and power than non-obligatory prayers?

". . . the obligatory prayers are by their very nature of greater effectiveness and are endowed with a greater power than the non-obligatory ones. . . ." (On behalf of Shoghi Effendi, *Spiritual Foundations* #41)

5. What is the significance of the words and movements of the obligatory prayer?

"Know thou that in every word and movement of the obligatory prayer there are allusions, mysteries and a wisdom that man is unable to comprehend, and letters and scrolls cannot contain."

('Abdu'l-Bahá, *Spiritual Foundations* #27)

"Bahá'u'lláh has reduced all ritual and form to an absolute minimum in His Faith. The few forms that there are—like those associated with the two longer obligatory daily prayers, are only symbols of the inner attitude. There is a wisdom in them, and a great blessing, but we cannot force ourselves to understand or feel these things, that is why He gave us also the very short and simple prayer, for those who did not feel the desire to perform the acts associated with the other two."

(On behalf of Shoghi Effendi, Spiritual Foundations #59)

6. Are there certain times when prayer is more effective?

"Occupy thyself in remembrance of the Beauty of Him Who is the Unconstrained, at early morn and seek communion with Him at the hour of dawn." (Bahá'u'lláh, Spiritual Foundations #11)

"Prayer verily bestoweth life, particularly when offered in private and at times, such as midnight, when freed from daily cares."

(Selections from the Writings of 'Abdu'l-Bahá, p. 202)

Illustration

"When 'Abdu'l-Bahá was in New York, He called to Him an ardent Bahá'í and said, 'If you will come to Me at dawn tomorrow, I will teach you to pray.'

"Delighted, Mr M arose at four and crossed the city, arriving for his lesson at six. With what exultant expectation he must have greeted this opportunity! He found 'Abdu'l-Bahá already at prayer, kneeling by the side of the bed. Mr M followed suit, taking care to place himself directly across.

"Seeing that 'Abdu'l-Bahá was quite lost in His Own reverie, Mr M began to pray silently for his friends, his family and finally for the crowned heads of Europe. No word was uttered by the quiet Man before him. He went over all the prayers he knew then, and repeated them twice, three times—still no sound broke the expectant hush.

"Mr M surreptitiously rubbed one knee and wondered vaguely about his back. He began again, hearing as he did so, the birds heralding the dawn outside the window. An hour passed, and finally two. Mr M was quite numb now. His eyes, roving along the wall, caught sight of a large crack. He dallied with a touch of indignation but let his gaze pass again to the still figure across the bed.

19

"The ecstasy that he saw arrested him and he drank deeply of the sight. Suddenly he wanted to pray like that. Selfish desires were forgotten. Sorrow, conflict, and even his immediate surroundings were as if they had never been. He was conscious of only one thing, a passionate desire to draw near to God.

"Closing his eyes again he set the world firmly aside, and amazingly his heart teemed with prayer, eager, joyous, tumultuous prayer. He felt cleansed by humility and lifted by a new peace. 'Abdu'l-Bahá had taught him to pray!

"The 'Master of 'Akká' immediately arose and came to him. His eyes rested smilingly upon the newly humbled Mr M. 'When you pray,' He said, 'you must not think of your aching body, nor of the birds outside the window, nor the cracks in the wall!'

"He became very serious then, and added, 'When you wish to pray you must first know that you are standing in the presence of the Almighty!'" (*Vignettes from the Life of 'Abdu'l-Bahá*, pp. 131-32)

Study References

1. The three Obligatory Prayers are included among the "Supplementary Texts" in the *Kitáb-i-Aqdas*, are printed in *Prayers and Meditations*, pp. 314-23, may be found in most Bahá'í prayer books, and have been reprinted in Appendix A.

2. Explanations of some of the features and movements of the Obligatory Prayers are contained in the footnotes in Appendix A.

3. For additional details regarding obligatory prayer, see the *Kitáb-i-Aqdas*.

4. *Prayers and Meditations* contains numerous prayers by Bahá'u'lláh. Prayers by Bahá'u'lláh, the Báb, and 'Abdu'l-Bahá may be found in the book *Bahá'í Prayers*.

5. For more on the nature of prayer, see the compilation entitled *Spiritual Foundations: Prayer, Meditation, and the Devotional Attitude*.

Reciting the Verses of God and Meditation

"Peruse ye every day the verses revealed by God.
Blessed is the man who reciteth them and reflecteth upon them."[68]
—Bahá'u'lláh

Reciting the Verses of God

An essential spiritual practice ordained by Bahá'u'lláh is recitation of the holy verses, at least two times each day: "Recite ye the verses of God every morn and eventide."[69] What are the "verses of God"? Bahá'u'lláh states that it refers to "all that hath been sent down from the Heaven of Divine Utterance."[70] The term "verses of God" does not include the Writings of 'Abdu'l-Bahá or Shoghi Effendi.[71] Does the term include the Writings of the Báb? In a letter on behalf of the Universal House of Justice, it has been written, "nothing has been found in the Writings of the Faith which specifically answers your question as to whether the Writings of the Báb are included among those verses recited 'every morn and eventide'. Thus you should feel free to come to your own conclusion as to whether or not you will include the Writings of the Báb in observing this particular injunction of the Kitáb-i-Aqdas."[72]

Reciting the verses of God should not be considered the same practice as study of the Faith (discussed in the next chapter). These are two distinct spiritual practices. It is the "verses of God" that are recited each morning and evening; whereas, study of the Faith involves reading all of the Faith's authoritative Writings, which include those of Bahá'u'lláh,

21

the Báb, 'Abdu'l-Bahá, Shoghi Effendi, and the Universal House of Justice. Study of the Faith also involves studying the history of the Faith, its relationship to various systems of thought, and the application of its Teachings to the spiritual and material life of society.[73] Further, reciting the holy verses is carried out at special times, every morning and evening; study may be done at any time. Moreover, "reciting" may imply the reading or repeating of verses out loud.

In what spirit should the verses of God be recited? Bahá'u'lláh has revealed that the "prime requisite" for reciting the verses of God is "the eagerness and love of sanctified souls to read the Word of God."[74] He further has said that "were a man to read a single verse with joy and radiance it would be better for him than to read with lassitude all the Holy Books of God. . . ."[75] While reciting the verses of God, the believer should also strive for such qualities as "reverence, attention and thought."[76] Bahá'u'lláh warns that whoever fails to recite the verses of God "hath not been faithful to the Covenant of God and His Testament."[77]

Reciting the verses of God is not just an individual practice, but, ideally, should become a daily family activity.[78] In addition to having a positive impact on the spiritual development of individual family members, this activity would be a powerful means of increasing the unity of the family.

The Bahá'í Writings also encourage us to commit the verses of God to memory.

Meditation

Another spiritual practice set forth in the Bahá'í Writings is meditation. Meditation is closely related not only to reciting the verses of God, but also to prayer, study, and action. 'Abdu'l-Bahá has described meditation as conversation with one's own soul: "In that state of mind you put certain questions to your spirit and the spirit answers: the light breaks forth and the reality is revealed."[79] He further describes meditation as "the key for opening the doors of mysteries. In that state man abstracts himself: in that state man withdraws himself from all outside objects; in that subjective mood he is immersed in the ocean of spiritual life and can unfold the secrets of things-in-themselves."[80]

He warns, however, that some thoughts are "useless" like "waves moving in the sea without result. But if the faculty of meditation is bathed in the inner light and characterized with divine attributes, the results will be confirmed."[81] Therefore, "The inspiration received through meditation is of a nature that one cannot measure or determine. God can inspire into our minds things that we had no previous knowledge of, if He desires to do so."[82] Because we cannot know for sure whether a meditative thought is truly inspired or "useless," it is good to weigh it against the standards of the Faith's Teachings.

The faculty of meditation is like a mirror. If it is put before earthly objects, the reflection will be earthly. On the other hand, if it is turned towards heaven and things of the spirit, then that is what will be reflected during meditation.[83] It is for this reason that the Guardian has encouraged us when meditating to use the words of Bahá'u'lláh and 'Abdu'l-Bahá.[84] We may meditate on any passage in the Writings. Moreover, there are many passages that specifically use words such as "meditate," "ponder," "reflect," and "consider," to direct us to meditate about specific themes or principles.

Like the daily obligatory prayers, meditation is "a private individual activity, not a form of group therapy."[85] Beyond the general principles discussed in the Writings, we are taught that there are "no set forms of meditation prescribed in the teachings."[86] Individuals are "free to do as they wish in this area, provided that they remain in harmony with the teachings."[87]

Quotations for Reflection

1. What are the consequences of failing to recite the verses of God every morning and evening?

"Recite ye the verses of God every morn and eventide. Whoso faileth to recite them hath not been faithful to the Covenant of God and His Testament, and whoso turneth away from these holy verses in this Day is of those who throughout eternity have turned away from God."

(Bahá'u'lláh, *Kitáb-i-Aqdas*, parag. 149)

2. What is the significance and power of the Word of God?

"The Word of God is the king of words and its pervasive influence is incalculable. It hath ever dominated and will continue to dominate the realm of being. The Great Being saith: The Word is the master key for the whole world, inasmuch as through its potency the doors of the hearts of men, which in reality are the doors of heaven, are unlocked.... It is an ocean inexhaustible in riches, comprehending all things."

(Tablets of Bahá'u'lláh, p. 173)

"Every word that proceedeth out of the mouth of God is endowed with such potency as can instill new life into every human frame, if ye be of them that comprehend this truth."

(Gleanings from the Writings of Bahá'u'lláh, p. 141)

3. What are the effects when a person, in the privacy of his chamber, recites the verses revealed by God?

"Whoso reciteth, in the privacy of his chamber, the verses revealed by God, the scattering angels of the Almighty shall scatter abroad the fragrance of the words uttered by his mouth, and shall cause the heart of every righteous man to throb. Though he may, at first, remain unaware of its effect, yet the virtue of the grace vouchsafed unto him must needs sooner or later exercise its influence upon his soul. Thus have the mysteries of the Revelation of God been decreed by virtue of the Will of Him Who is the Source of power and wisdom."

(Gleanings from the Writings of Bahá'u'lláh, p. 295)

4. Is the recital of the *Hidden Words*, revealed by Bahá'u'lláh, recommended?

"It behoveth us one and all to recite day and night both the Persian and Arabic *Hidden Words*, to pray fervently and supplicate tearfully that we may be enabled to conduct ourselves in accordance with these divine counsels. These holy Words have not been revealed to be heard but to be practiced." ('Abdu'l-Bahá, *Deepening* #37)

"Be assured in thyself that if thou dost conduct thyself in accordance with the *Hidden Words* revealed in Persian and in Arabic, thou

24

shalt become a torch of fire of the love of God, an embodiment of humility, of lowliness, of evanescence and of selflessness."

('Abdu'l-Bahá, *Deepening* #39)

5. What are the results of meditating on that which Bahá'u'lláh has revealed?

"Do thou meditate on that which We have revealed unto thee, that thou mayest discover the purpose of God, thy Lord, and the Lord of all worlds. In these words the mysteries of Divine Wisdom have been treasured." (*Gleanings from the Writings of Bahá'u'lláh*, p. 153)

"Were any man to ponder in his heart that which the Pen of the Most High hath revealed and to taste of its sweetness, he would, of a certainty, find himself emptied and delivered from his own desires, and utterly subservient to the Will of the Almighty. Happy is the man that hath attained so high a station, and hath not deprived himself of so bountiful a grace." (*Gleanings from the Writings of Bahá'u'lláh*, p. 343)

6. How should we meditate?

". . . There are no set forms of meditation prescribed in the teachings, no plan, as such, for inner development. The friends are urged— nay enjoined—to pray, and they also should meditate, but the manner of doing the latter is left entirely to the individual. . . ."

(On behalf of Shoghi Effendi, *Spiritual Foundations* #50)

"He thinks it would be wiser for the Bahá'ís to use the Meditations given by Bahá'u'lláh, and not any set form of meditation recommended by someone else. . . ."

(On behalf of Shoghi Effendi, *Spiritual Foundations* #61)

"The House of Justice suggests that for their private meditations they [the believers] may wish to use the repetition of the Greatest Name, Alláh'u'Abhá, ninety-five times a day which, although not yet applied in the west, is among the Laws, Ordinances and Exhortations of the Kitáb-i-Aqdas."

(On behalf of the Universal House of Justice, *Lights of Guidance*, p. 541)

7. Prayer and meditation must go along with what?

"Chant the Words of God and, pondering over their meaning, transform them into actions!"　　　　('Abdu'l-Bahá, *Deepening* #51)

"Prayer and meditation are very important factors in deepening the spiritual life of the individual, but with them must go also action and example, as these are the tangible results of the former. Both are essential."　　　(On behalf of Shoghi Effendi, *Spiritual Foundations* #51)

Illustration

"One day the Guardian said to a prominent pilgrim in Haifa, 'Do you pray?' 'Of course, beloved Guardian, I pray every morning.' 'Do you meditate?' The man paused a bit and said slowly, 'No, I guess I do not.' The Guardian replied that prayer is of no use without meditation and that meditation must be centered on the Writings. He continued very earnestly that meditation is of no use unless it is followed by action. He thus made clear another step to this most important process in the life of the soul.

"The Guardian then explained further that meditation is not just sitting down, closing your eyes, keeping silent in a silent atmosphere, and being blank. That is not meditation. We must concentrate on the teachings, concentrate on their implications and how they can be used. Prayer is of no consequence if it remains the murmur of syllables and sounds—of what use is that? God knows already. We are not saying the prayers for God, we are saying them for our own selves. If the words do not strengthen us, if we do not reflect upon the Writings we read, if we do not make the Writings part of our daily action, we are wasting our time."　　　(Ruth J. Moffett, *Du'á: On Wings of Prayer*, p. 29)

Study References

1. For meditations revealed by Bahá'u'lláh, see *Prayers and Meditations*. In a letter written on his behalf, Shoghi Effendi stated that he had "every hope that the perusal of such a precious volume [*Prayers and Meditations*] will help to deepen, *more than any other publication*, the spirit of

devotion and faith in the friends, and thus charge them with all the spiritual power they require for the accomplishment of their tremendous duties towards the Cause."[88]

2. For more on the subject of meditation, see the compilation entitled *Spiritual Foundations: Prayer, Meditation, and the Devotional Attitude.*

3. For a daily readings book containing passages from the Writings of Bahá'u'lláh, see *Reciting the Verses of God: Spiritual Virtues and Practices.*

Study of the Faith

"Immerse yourselves in the ocean of My words,
that ye may unravel its secrets,
and discover all the pearls of wisdom that lie hid in its depths."[89]
—Bahá'u'lláh

The Spiritual Act of Study

The "first obligation and the object of the constant endeavor" of every Bahá'í should be to "strive to obtain a more adequate understanding of the significance of Bahá'u'lláh's stupendous Revelation."[90] Each Bahá'í, therefore, has the obligation to deepen his understanding of the Faith. What is primarily meant by "deepening" or study of the Faith? It is a clearer understanding "of the purpose of God for man, and particularly of His immediate purpose as revealed and directed by Bahá'u'lláh, a purpose as far removed from current concepts of human well-being and happiness as is possible."[91]

Why is study important? The Writings tell us that the "attainment of the most great guidance is dependent upon knowledge and wisdom, and on being informed as to the mysteries of the Holy Words. Wherefore must the loved ones of God, be they young or old, be they men or women, each one according to his capabilities, strive to acquire the various branches of knowledge, and to increase his understanding of the mysteries of the Holy Books, and his skill in marshalling the divine proofs and evidences."[92] Study of the verses "will attract you unto God and will enable you to detach yourselves from all else save Him."[93] Finally, 'Abdu'l-Bahá makes this remarkable statement about the spiritual consequences of study: "In this day there is nothing more important

29

than the instruction and study of clear proofs and convincing, heavenly arguments, for therein lie the source of life and the path of salvation."[94]

Studying the Faith is not simply a matter of acquiring information. It is a process of achieving divine knowledge and spiritual understanding. This process involves spiritual attitudes and qualities. For example, Bahá'u'lláh has written that the understanding and comprehension of the Words of God "are in no wise dependent upon human learning. They depend solely upon purity of heart, chastity of soul, and freedom of spirit."[95] Furthermore, "When your hearts are wholly attracted to the one true God you will acquire divine knowledge, will become attentive to the proofs and testimonies and will commit to memory the glad-tidings concerning the Manifestation of the Beauty of the All-Merciful, as mentioned in the heavenly Scriptures."[96]

We study the Bahá'í Teachings not only that we may understand them more deeply and fulfill them more faithfully, but that we may convey them more accurately to others.[97] In fact, study and teaching have a very close relationship: "To study and to teach, these are the twofold and sacred obligations of every responsible and active follower of the Faith."[98] Further, "A true and adequate knowledge of the Cause is, indeed, indispensable to everyone who wishes to successfully teach the Message."[99] As we study, we become more effective teachers, and as we teach, we gain deeper insights into the Faith and further inspiration to study it more intensely.

What and How to Study

What is it that we should study? The Universal House of Justice has explained that the study of the Faith includes "systematic study of the Writings of the Faith, its history, its relationship to various systems of thought, and the application of its Teachings to the spiritual and material life of society."[100] The Writings of the Central Figures of the Faith (Bahá'u'lláh, the Báb, and 'Abdu'l-Bahá) are Sacred Scripture: ". . . the term 'Sacred Scriptures' applies to the words of all the Manifestations of God together with the writings of 'Abdu'l-Bahá. . . ."[101] The writings of Shoghi Effendi and the Universal House of Justice, "though they are not regarded as sacred texts nor are of the same station as the Writings of the Central Figures of the Faith, nevertheless . . . are authoritative statements of guidance and direction for the friends."[102] Thus, only the authentic Writings of the Faith's three Central Figures, and those of Shoghi Effendi and the Universal House of Justice have binding authority over Bahá'ís. Hearsay or reported utterances, although of interest, can in no way claim authority.[103] Of course, the writings of individual believers are not authoritative, no matter how prominent a Bahá'í the author may be.

A listing of most of the authoritative Writings presently available in English is included in Appendix B. Of these Writings, certain ones are of special importance. For example, the *Kitáb-i-Aqdas* is the "Most Holy Book." Other works that Bahá'ís should master include the *Kitáb-i-Íqán, Gleanings from the Writings of Bahá'u'lláh, Tablets of Bahá'u'lláh,* the *Will and Testament of 'Abdu'l-Bahá, Some Answered Questions, God Passes By,* and *The Dawn-Breakers.*[104] Also, of particular importance is a letter by the Guardian entitled "The Dispensation of Bahá'u'lláh" (contained in the book *The World Order of Bahá'u'lláh*), in which he explains "the fundamental verities of the Faith,"[105] "certain truths which lie at the basis of our Faith."[106]

In addition to the study of books, the "principles of the Teachings of Bahá'u'lláh should be carefully studied, one by one, until they are realized and understood by mind and heart. . . ."[107] Moreover, some of the important subjects and themes that we should study include the history of the Faith, the twin Covenants of Bahá'u'lláh and of 'Abdu'l-Bahá, the Administrative Order, the future World Order, the laws of the *Kitáb-i-Aqdas*, the institutions of the Guardianship and the Universal House of Justice, and the relationship of the Faith to past religions. We should also consider the following in our study: "What is Bahá'u'lláh's purpose for the human race? For what ends did He submit to the appalling cruelties and indignities heaped upon Him? What does He mean by 'a new race of men'? What are the profound changes which He will bring about? The answers are to be found in the Sacred Writings of our Faith and in their interpretation by 'Abdu'l-Bahá and our beloved Guardian."[108]

How should we carry out our study? Our study needs to be "systematic." It should be orderly, not random or haphazard. The major texts of Bahá'u'lláh, the Báb, 'Abdu'l-Bahá, Shoghi Effendi, and the Universal House of Justice presently available in English make up approximately thirty-five books. If a Bahá'í simply reads sixteen pages every day, over the course of a year, he can complete *every one* of these books! In addition to reading, we should carefully study these Writings, thinking about their implications and application. 'Abdu'l-Bahá has said that we should "investigate and study the Holy Scriptures word by word" so that we "may attain knowledge of the mysteries hidden therein." He continues, "Be not satisfied with words, but seek to understand the spiritual meanings hidden in the heart of the words."[109] (Appendix C presents some practical ideas on how to study the Writings.)

An important aspect of our study is to relate the Bahá'í Teachings to current issues facing humanity. How do the truths revealed by Bahá'u'lláh bear on the current thoughts and problems of the people around us? How do His principles help to solve these problems? "If the Bahá'ís want to be really effective in teaching the Cause they need to be much better informed and able to discuss intelligently, intellectually, the present condition of the world and its problems."[110] Bahá'u'lláh, as the Divine Physician, has given the remedy for the ills of humanity. We must learn what this remedy is and how we can apply it to the problems of our day.

Quotations for Reflection

1. What does it mean to deepen in the Cause?

"To deepen in the Cause means to read the writings of Bahá'u'lláh and the Master so thoroughly as to be able to give it to others in its pure form. There are many who have some superficial idea of what the Cause stands for. They, therefore, present it together with all sorts of ideas that are their own. As the Cause is still in its early days we must be most careful lest we fall under this error and injure the Movement we so much adore.

"There is no limit to the study of the Cause. The more we read the writings the more truths we can find in them and the more we will see that our previous notions were erroneous."

(On behalf of Shoghi Effendi, *Deepening* #93)

2. What is the purpose of reading of the scriptures and holy books?

". . . the reading of the scriptures and holy books is for no other purpose except to enable the reader to apprehend their meaning and unravel their innermost mysteries. Otherwise reading, without understanding, is of no abiding profit unto man."

(Bahá'u'lláh, *Kitáb-i-Íqán*, p. 172)

3. In proportion to what, does the seeker partake of the benefits preordained in God's Tablets?

"My holy, My divinely ordained Revelation may be likened unto an ocean in whose depths are concealed innumerable pearls of great price, of surpassing luster. It is the duty of every seeker to bestir himself and strive to attain the shores of this ocean, so that he may, in proportion to the eagerness of his search and the efforts he hath exerted, partake of such benefits as have been preordained in God's irrevocable and hidden Tablets. If no one be willing to direct his steps towards its shores, if every one should fail to arise and find Him, can such a failure be said to have robbed this ocean of its power or to have lessened, to any degree, its treasures?" (*Gleanings from the Writings of Bahá'u'lláh*, p. 326)

4. What would be the result in our lives if we immersed ourselves in and fathomed the depths of the ocean of Bahá'u'lláh's teachings?

"Indeed if an avowed follower of Bahá'u'lláh were to immerse himself in, and fathom the depths of, the ocean of these heavenly teachings, and with utmost care and attention deduce from each of them the subtle mysteries and consummate wisdom that lie enshrined therein, such a person's life, materially, intellectually and spiritually, will be safe from toil and trouble, and unaffected by setbacks and perils, or any sadness or despondency." (Shoghi Effendi, *Deepening* #69)

"If you read the utterances of Bahá'u'lláh and 'Abdu'l-Bahá with selflessness and care and concentrate upon them, you will discover truths unknown to you before and will obtain an insight into the problems that have baffled the great thinkers of the world."

(Shoghi Effendi, *Deepening* #72)

5. What can just one mature soul, with spiritual understanding and a profound knowledge of the Faith, achieve?

"Just one mature soul, with spiritual understanding and a profound knowledge of the Faith, can set a whole country ablaze—so great is the power of the Cause to work through a pure and selfless channel."

(On behalf of Shoghi Effendi, *Deepening* #155)

6. Young Bahá'ís should gain a mastery of what books?

". . . as to what subjects within the Faith you should concentrate on he feels that the young Bahá'ís should gain a mastery of such books as the *Gleanings*, the *Dawnbreakers*, *God Passes By*, the *Íqán*, *Some Answered Questions* and the more important Tablets. All aspects of the Faith should be deeply studied. . . ."   (On behalf of Shoghi Effendi, *Deepening* #143)

7. What is the definition of a Bahá'í scholar?

"The Cause needs more Bahá'í scholars, people who not only are devoted to it and believe in it and are anxious to tell others about it, but also who have a deep grasp of the teachings and their significance, and who can correlate its beliefs with the current thoughts and problems of the people of the world.

"The Cause has the remedy for all the world's ills. The reason why more people don't accept it is because the Bahá'ís are not always capable of presenting it to them in a way that meets the immediate needs of their minds."   (On behalf of Shoghi Effendi, *Deepening* #137)

"We need Bahá'í scholars, not only people far, far more deeply aware of what our teachings really are, but also well read and well educated people, capable of correlating our teachings to the current thoughts of the leaders of society."   (On behalf of Shoghi Effendi, *Deepening* #153)

Illustration

"Perhaps it may be helpful at this time to speak of the effects which the mere reading of these divine Words has produced in my own life, and the lives of many others to whom I have been privileged to introduce this new Revelation. . . . Over and over again I have seen hearts illumined and lives transformed by merely reading a few passages from *The Hidden Words*, or the *Tablet to the Pope*, or *The Book of Certitude*, or the *Surat-'l-Hykl* [a tablet by Bahá'u'lláh], or, in fact, from any of the books opened at random. Through these Words, indeed, 'Flows the River of Divine Knowledge and bursts the Fire of the Consummate Wisdom of the Eternal.' For something like five years after meeting the Master ['Abdu'l-Bahá] I literally read nothing else. I crossed the continent twice during those years and carried with me a satchel filled with these books and typed copies of Tablets, which I studied constantly on the train and elsewhere. I became soaked in the 'Oceans of Divine Utterance.' To this fact alone, accompanied with constant prayer, may be ascribed whatever slight progress may have been made in the Pathway of Eternal Life. The heavenly Significances, these 'pearls hidden in the depths of the Ocean of His Verses,' have opened portals to a freedom of mind and spirit such as no writings of human genius have ever bestowed. That there is a Power flowing from these Words capable of bestowing 'a new life of faith' there has to me been abundant proof."

(Howard Colby Ives, *Portals to Freedom*, pp. 77-78)

Study References

1. For more on the study of the Writings, see the compilation entitled *Deepening* (or *The Importance of Deepening our Knowledge and Understanding of the Faith*).

2. For a listing of the Authoritative Writings of the Faith and summaries of the contents of these texts, see Appendix B. For a listing of compilations of quotations from the Bahá'í Writings on various subjects, see Appendix B.

3. For information on how to order Bahá'í books, see Appendix B.

4. For practical ideas on how to study the Bahá'í Writings, see Appendix C. The books *The Word of God* and *Reading Bahá'u'lláh's Word* are additional materials available for study about the Creative Word.

Teaching the Faith

*"Verily, We behold you from Our realm of glory,
and shall aid whosoever will arise for the triumph of Our Cause. . . ."*[111]
—Bahá'u'lláh

The Spiritual Act of Teaching

Humanity is suffering from the ills of immorality, prejudice, hatred, disunity, selfishness, tyranny, and lack of trustworthiness. The Faith of Bahá'u'lláh is the divine remedy for this suffering. It is a remedy that brings about unity, spirituality, and happiness. Those of us who have accepted the Faith have begun to apply that remedy to our own lives. However, the vast majority of humanity is still not aware that this healing medicine exists. In order to bring an end to humanity's agony, we must share the knowledge of Bahá'u'lláh's remedy with those who are still unaware of it. This act of sharing the Message of the Bahá'í Faith with others is teaching.

Bahá'u'lláh has called every Bahá'í to the sacred privilege and obligation of teaching: "Teach ye the Cause of God, O people of Bahá, for God hath prescribed unto every one the duty of proclaiming His Message, and regardeth it as the most meritorious of all deeds."[112] He has promised His assistance and blessings to every follower who arises to teach: "He, verily, will aid everyone that aideth Him, and will remember everyone that remembereth Him."[113] What is the result if we neglect the duty to teach? The Writings make it clear that "in this day, confirmations from the unseen world are encompassing all those who deliver the divine Message. Should the work of teaching lapse, these confirmations would be entirely cut off, since it is impossible for the loved ones of God to receive assistance unless they teach."[114]

Teaching the Faith is not simply a matter of conveying information to others. It is a spiritual process that requires spiritual preparation and action. The teacher must possess certain spiritual qualities in order that his words may affect others. 'Abdu'l-Bahá has written, "The intention of the teacher must be pure, his heart independent, his spirit attracted, his thought at peace, his resolution firm, his magnanimity exalted and in the love of God a shining torch. Should he become as such, his sanctified breath will even affect the rock; otherwise there will be no result whatsoever. As long as a soul is not perfected, how can he efface the defects of others?"[115] Other qualities that the teacher must possess include detachment, love, selflessness, humility, kindliness, righteousness, dedication, knowledge, and wisdom.

Should we wait until we possess all of these qualities and until we are fully qualified before we teach? The Guardian has answered this question: "If the friends always waited until they were *fully* qualified to do any particular task, the work of the Cause would be almost at a standstill! But the very act of striving to serve, however unworthy one may feel, attracts the blessings of God and enables one to become more fitted for the task."[116] "Thus the best way to develop capacity in teaching the Faith, is to teach. As one teaches, he gains more knowledge himself, he relies more on the guidance of the spirit, and expands his own character."[117]

Therefore, we cannot excuse ourselves by saying, "I don't know enough about the Faith to teach others." No Bahá'í will ever have enough knowledge of the Faith. We must teach others on the basis of what we have read and learned. As we study the Writings more, our presentation of the Faith will improve. If we are asked a question we cannot answer, we can simply reply, "I don't know," or "I have not yet studied that aspect of the Faith, but I will investigate and find the answer for you," or "Let's see if we can discover the answer together."

Practical Approaches to Teaching

In addition to emphasizing spiritual preparation, the Writings also provide guidance to the teacher on what methods to pursue and what actions to carry out. The believer "must concentrate his thoughts on teaching."[118] He should ponder and meditate regarding the methods of teaching,[119] and consider all approaches he might use in "his personal attempts to capture the attention, maintain the interest, and deepen the faith, of those whom he seeks to bring into the fold of his Faith. Let him survey the possibilities which the particular circumstances in which he lives offer him, evaluate their advantages, and proceed intelligently and systematically to utilize them for the achievement of the object he has in mind."[120]

Whom should we teach? Bahá'u'lláh says, "Proclaim the Cause of thy Lord unto all who are in the heavens and on the earth. Should any man respond to thy call, lay bare before him the pearls of the wisdom of the Lord...."[121] 'Abdu'l-Bahá writes, "The friends of God should weave bonds of fellowship with others and show absolute love and affection towards them. These links have a deep influence on people and they will listen. When the friends sense receptivity to the Word of God, they should deliver the Message with wisdom."[122] Further, "the most effective way for the Bahá'ís to teach the Faith is to make strong friends with their neighbors and associates. When the friends have confidence in the Bahá'ís and the Bahá'ís in their friends, they should give the Message and teach the Cause. Individual teaching of this type is more effective than any other type."[123]

When we teach, what should we say? "From the texts of the wondrous, heavenly Scriptures they should memorize phrases and passages bearing on various instances, so that in the course of their speech they may recite divine verses whenever the occasion demandeth it...."[124] "It is very good to memorize the logical points and the proofs of the Holy Books.... As soon as someone will ask you—What are your proofs?— you may cry out at the top of your voice and say: 'Here they are!'"[125]

The able teacher does not give everyone the same presentation of the Teachings, but adapts his methods to the spiritual needs of the listener: "First diagnose the disease and identify the malady, then prescribe the remedy...."[126] For example, "Those who are essentially of the mystic type should first be given those teachings of the Cause which emphasize the nature and value of spiritual realities; while those who are practically minded and of a positive type are naturally more ready and inclined to accept the social aspect of the Teachings. But of course, gradually the *entire* Message, in all its aspects and with the full implications it entails, should be explained to the newcomer."[127] Accordingly, listening to the seeker and understanding his "character and mind"[128] are essential to successful teaching.

The teacher should also bear in mind that although he must teach with courage, he should never coerce or bring undue pressure on inquirers: "The path to guidance is one of love and compassion, not of force and coercion."[129] "If ye be aware of a certain truth, if ye possess a jewel, of which others are deprived, share it with them in a language of utmost kindliness and goodwill. If it be accepted, it if fulfil its purpose, your object is attained. If any one should refuse it, leave him unto himself, and beseech God to guide him."[130] Bahá'u'lláh further writes, "Help him to see and recognize the truth, without esteeming yourself to be, in the least, superior to him, or to be possessed of greater endowments."[131] Thus, teaching is like humbly offering a precious gift to a friend.

One of the most effective methods of teaching is for the believer to invite friends to his home for the purpose of introducing them to the Faith and sharing with them this cherished aspect of his life. "Close association and loving service affects the hearts; and when the heart is affected, then the spirit can enter."[132] In such an informal atmosphere, the questions of the inquirer can be answered, and those aspects of the Faith that are of particular interest to him can be discussed. The Guardian has stated that every believer should have such a teaching gathering in his home at least once each Bahá'í month. 'Abdu'l-Bahá's statement, that every Bahá'í should lead at least one person to the Faith each year, provides another individual teaching goal.

Finally, "Having . . . obtained a clear understanding of the true character of our mission, the methods to adopt, the course to pursue, and having attained sufficiently the individual regeneration—the essential requisite of teaching—let us arise to teach His Cause with righteousness, conviction, understanding and vigor. Let this be the paramount and most urgent duty of every Bahá'í. Let us make it the dominating passion of our life."[133] Our teaching efforts will succeed if we constantly rely on the power of Bahá'u'lláh and if we arise to fulfill the sacred words of 'Abdu'l-Bahá:

> In these days, the most important of all things is the guidance of the nations and peoples of the world. Teaching the Cause is of utmost importance for it is the head cornerstone of the foun-

dation itself. This wronged servant has spent his days and nights in promoting the Cause and urging the peoples to service. He rested not a moment, till the fame of the Cause of God was noised abroad in the world and the celestial strains from the Abhá Kingdom roused the East and the West. The beloved of God must also follow the same example. This is the secret of faithfulness, this is the requirement of servitude to the Threshold of Bahá![134]

Quotations for Reflection

1. What are the bounties of teaching?

"It is better to guide one soul than to possess all that is on earth, for as long as that guided soul is under the shadow of the Tree of Divine Unity, he and the one who hath guided him will both be recipients of God's tender mercy, whereas possession of earthly things will cease at the time of death." (*Selections from the Writings of the Báb*, p. 77)

"Of all the gifts of God the greatest is the gift of Teaching. It draweth unto us the Grace of God and is our first obligation."
(*Will and Testament of 'Abdu'l-Bahá*, p. 25)

2. What makes one a "best teacher" and an "exemplary believer"?

"A 'best teacher' and an 'exemplary believer' is ultimately neither more nor less than an ordinary Bahá'í who has consecrated himself to the work of the Faith, deepened his knowledge and understanding of its Teachings, placed his confidence in Bahá'u'lláh, and arisen to serve Him to the best of his ability. This door is one which we are assured will open before the face of every follower of the Faith who knocks hard enough, so to speak. When the will and the desire are strong enough, the means will be found and the way opened. . . ."
(On behalf of Shoghi Effendi, *The Individual and Teaching* #116)

3. What is the most effective way for the Bahá'ís to teach?

"The Bahá'ís must realize that the success of this work depends upon the individual. The individual must arise as never before to proclaim the Faith of Bahá'u'lláh. The most effective way for them to carry on their work is for the individual to make many contacts, select a few who they feel would become Bahá'ís, develop a close friendship with them, then complete confidence, and finally teach them the Faith, until they become strong supporters of the Cause of God."

(On behalf of Shoghi Effendi, *The Individual and Teaching* #95)

4. What must we do to find souls who are receptive to the Faith?

"... make a special point of praying ardently not only for success in general, but that God may send to you the souls that are ready. There are such souls in every city. . . ."

(On behalf of Shoghi Effendi, *The Individual and Teaching* #78)

"Teaching the Faith is not conditioned by what occupation we have, or how great our knowledge is, but rather on how much we have studied the Teachings, to what degree we live the Bahá'í life, and how much we long to share this Message with others. When we have these characteristics, we are sure, if we search, to find receptive souls."

(On behalf of Shoghi Effendi, *Lights of Guidance*, p. 585)

5. What must the teacher do in order for the heart of the seeker to be influenced?

"Whoso ariseth among you to teach the Cause of his Lord, let him, before all else, teach his own self, that his speech may attract the hearts of them that hear him. Unless he teacheth his own self, the words of his mouth will not influence the heart of the seeker."

(*Gleanings from the Writings of Bahá'u'lláh*, p. 277)

"God hath prescribed unto every one the duty of teaching His Cause. Whoever ariseth to discharge this duty, must needs, ere he proclaimeth His Message, adorn himself with the ornament of an upright and praiseworthy character, so that his words may attract the hearts of such as are receptive to his call. Without it, he can never hope to influence his hearers." (*Gleanings from the Writings of Bahá'u'lláh*, p. 335)

6. Is good conduct and advice on the part of the Bahá'ís sufficient in order for the Faith to advance?

"If their task is to be confined to good conduct and advice, nothing will be accomplished. They must speak out, expound the proofs, set forth clear arguments, draw irrefutable conclusions establishing the truth of the manifestation of the Sun of Reality."

(Selections from the Writings of 'Abdu'l-Bahá, p. 268)

7. What must the teacher do after he has taught a seeker?

"Let him. . . endeavor to nurse him, patiently, tactfully, and yet determinedly, into full maturity, and aid him to proclaim his unqualified acceptance of whatever has been ordained by Bahá'u'lláh. . . . Let him not be content until he has infused into his spiritual child so deep a longing as to impel him to arise independently, in his turn, and devote his energies to the quickening of other souls, and the upholding of the laws and principles laid down by his newly adopted Faith."

(Shoghi Effendi, *The Advent of Divine Justice*, p. 52)

"The Friends should seek pure souls, gain their confidence and then teach that person carefully until he becomes a Bahá'í—and then nurture him until he becomes a firm and active supporter of the Faith."

(On behalf of Shoghi Effendi, *The Individual and Teaching* #100)

"The purpose of teaching is not complete when a person declares that he has accepted Bahá'u'lláh as the Manifestation of God for this age; the purpose of teaching is to attract human beings to the Divine Message and so imbue them with its spirit that they will dedicate themselves to its service, and this world will become another world and its people another people. Viewed in this light a declaration of Faith is merely a milestone along the way—albeit a very important one. Teaching may also be likened to kindling a fire, the fire of faith, in the hearts of men. If a fire burns only so long as the match is held to it, it cannot truly be said to have been kindled; to be kindled it must continue to burn of its own accord."

(Universal House of Justice, *Lights of Guidance*, pp. 594-95)

Illustration

"In all of my many opportunities of meeting, of listening to and talking with 'Abdu'l-Bahá I was impressed, and constantly more deeply impressed, with His method of teaching souls. That is the word. He did not attempt to reach the mind alone. He sought the soul, the reality of every one He met. Oh, He could be logical, even scientific in His presentation of an argument, as He demonstrated constantly in the many addresses I have heard Him give and the many more I have read. But it was not the logic of the schoolman, not the science of the class room. His lightest word, His slightest association with a soul was shot through with an illuminating radiance which lifted the hearer to a higher plane of consciousness. Our hearts burned within us when He spoke. And He never argued, of course. Nor did he press a point. He left one free. There was never an assumption of authority, rather He was ever the personification of humility. He taught 'as if offering a gift to a king.' He never told me what I should do, beyond suggesting that what I was doing was right. Nor did He ever tell me what I should believe. He made Truth and Love so beautiful and royal that the heart perforce did reverence. He showed me by His voice, manner, bearing, smile, how I should *be*, knowing that out of the pure soil of being the good fruit of deeds and words would surely spring.

"There was a strange, awe-inspiring mingling of humility and majesty, relaxation and power in His slightest word or gesture which made me long to understand its source. What made Him so different, so immeasurably superior to any other man I had ever met?"

(Howard Colby Ives, *Portals to Freedom*, pp. 39-40)

Study References

1. The "Charter" for teaching is 'Abdu'l-Bahá's *Tablets of the Divine Plan*. Shoghi Effendi's explanations about teaching are contained in *The Advent of Divine Justice*. He also discusses in two other letters—"The Challenging Requirements of the Present Hour" and "American Bahá'ís in the Time of World Peril"—the teaching mission that 'Abdu'l-Bahá has given to American Bahá'ís. Both of these letters are contained in the book *Citadel of Faith*.

2. For a comprehensive compilation of quotations related to teaching, see *The Individual and Teaching* (*The Gift of Teaching*). See also the compilation entitled *The Power of Divine Assistance.* The training book *Raising The Call: The Individual and Effective Teaching* discusses some of the insights and skills necessary to effectively teach.

3. Bahá'í teachers should master the *Kitáb-i-Íqán (The Book of Certitude)* and *Some Answered Questions.* In the *Kitáb-i-Íqán*, Bahá'u'lláh explains basic teachings such as the unity of the Prophets and unravels the prophecies of the Bible and the Qur'án. In *Some Answered Questions*, 'Abdu'l-Bahá answers questions on more than eighty different subjects, ranging from proofs for the existence of God to the immortality of the soul; Christian topics, including the Resurrection, the Trinity, and the Second Coming; and other matters such as evolution, the nonexistence of evil, and reincarnation.

4. The study booklet *The Spiritual Conquest of the Planet* presents an overview of the systematic unfoldment of the Divine Plan through a series of International Teaching Plans and gives references describing the role of the individual and community in pursuing the goals of the Plans.

5. The compilation *The Proofs of Bahá'u'lláh's Mission* contains references from the authoritative texts establishing the truth of Bahá'u'lláh's claim.

6. For a practical method of teaching, see the discussion of teaching groups in Appendix D.

Observance of Divine Laws and Principles

"O Son of Being! Walk in My statutes for love of Me
and deny thyself that which thou desirest if thou seekest My pleasure."[135]
—Bahá'u'lláh

The first duty God has prescribed for man is to recognize the Manifestation of God. Whoever achieves this duty has "attained unto all good."[136] Man's second duty is to observe every ordinance set forth by God's Manifestation. "These twin duties are inseparable. Neither is acceptable without the other."[137] Because we, as Bahá'ís, have recognized Bahá'u'lláh as the Manifestation of God for this age, we must strive to obey His ordinances. Bahá'u'lláh's ordinances take the form of laws and principles. The sacred duties discussed in the other chapters of the present book are among the ordinances revealed by Bahá'u'lláh. This chapter discusses other significant ordinances.

The Laws and Principles of God

The *Kitáb-i-Aqdas* contains the laws that Bahá'ís must follow. Bahá'u'lláh warns in that book, "Think not that We have revealed unto you a mere code of laws."[138] "Know assuredly that My commandments are the lamps of My loving providence among My servants, and the keys of My mercy for My creatures."[139] As believers, we obey these laws because of our love for God. This obedience increases our love for, and knowledge of, God and allows us to grow closer to Him: "For man's knowledge of God cannot develop fully and adequately save by observing whatsoever hath been ordained by Him and is set forth in His heavenly Book."[140] One of the most important laws Bahá'u'lláh has ordained is the law of fasting. He has written, "We have commanded you to pray and fast from the beginning of maturity; this is ordained by God, your Lord and the Lord of your forefathers."[141] Fasting occupies "an exalted station in the sight of God."[142] What is the significance of fasting? 'Abdu'l-Bahá has explained, "For this material fast is an outer token of the spiritual fast; it is a symbol of self-restraint, the withholding of oneself from all appetites of the self, taking on the characteristics of the spirit, being carried away by the breathings of heaven and catching fire from the love of God."[143]

Bahá'ís fast during a specific time of the year, namely, the last month of the Bahá'í calendar. This month falls on March 2nd through March 20th of each year. Bahá'u'lláh has commanded His followers to abstain from food and drink from sunrise to sundown during each day of this nineteen-day period.[144] We are free to eat or drink before sunrise and after sundown. The fast is binding on men and women who have attained maturity, which is defined as 15 years of age.[145] Exemption from fasting is granted to those who are travelling, ill, over the age of 70, those who are engaged in heavy labor, and women who are pregnant or nursing.[146] Bahá'u'lláh states that God has bidden "all men to observe the fast, that through it they may purify their souls and rid themselves of all attachment to any one but Thee. . . ."[147]

Other laws which the Bahá'í Writings enjoin us to follow include:

1. engaging in a trade or profession
2. being obedient to government
3. providing for the education of one's children
4. not consuming alcohol or habit-forming drugs, such as marijuana, cocaine, LSD, etc. (unless prescribed by a qualified physician as part of a medical treatment)
5. not gambling
6. being chaste before marriage, and absolutely faithful during marriage
7. not backbiting or gossiping
8. not participating in partisan politics
9. obeying the Bahá'í laws on marriage

48

10. observing Bahá'í holy days (Work and school are suspended on these days. See Appendix F for a listing and explanation of the Bahá'í holy days.)

In addition to obeying the laws of Bahá'u'lláh, Bahá'ís also strive to behave in accord with His divine principles—spiritual attributes, standards, and virtues. The difference between a law and a principle may best be illustrated through an example: Saying one's obligatory prayer is a law, but being fair to others is a principle. The Faith's many principles, spiritual and social, appear throughout the Bahá'í Writings.

For instance, Bahá'u'lláh has written that the "goodliest vesture in the sight of God in this day is trustworthiness."[148] 'Abdu'l-Bahá states, "Truthfulness is the foundation of all human virtues."[149] Justice is described as the "best beloved of all things"[150] in God's sight. Further, "greater than all, after recognition of the unity of God . . . is regard for the rights that are due to one's parents."[151] Moreover, Bahá'ís must strive to be free from prejudices of all kinds and must work to ensure the equality of women and men. This is only a sampling of the many divine principles that one discovers through study of the Writings.

As the individual strives to behave in accordance with divine laws and principles, "transformative forces . . . operate upon his soul."[152] The "outcome" of this obedience is "acquisition of spiritual and moral character."[153]

Steadfastness in Obedience

One of the important concepts to keep in mind as we strive to observe the laws and principles of God is that we live in two different worlds simultaneously. We live in the physical world that we can perceive with our senses. At the same time, we live in the spiritual world that we cannot see, hear, or touch. We can sometimes know the physical consequences of our actions, but on our own, we do not know the spiritual consequences of our actions. For example, if a person backbites or criticizes another, from a physical perspective, this is simply the utterance of words caused by the movement of the tongue and lips. From a spiritual perspective, however, the reciting of these words of criticism has great destructive spiritual results.

Bahá'u'lláh has written that "backbiting quencheth the light of the heart, and extinguisheth the life of the soul."[154] Further, "Material fire consumeth the body, whereas the fire of the tongue devoureth both heart and soul. The force of the former lasteth but for a time, whilst the effects of the latter endure a century."[155] Thus, the seemingly harmless act of saying a few words of criticism has terrible spiritual consequences of which we may not have been aware. The way we can learn about the spiritual consequences of our actions is by turning towards the laws and principles of Bahá'u'lláh. He has directed us to perform those actions that spiritually benefit us and forbidden those that are spiritually harmful.

Therefore, we should be constant and steadfast in carrying out the divine laws and principles, even though we may not at first see their wisdom. In studying the Faith, every believer will, sooner or later, encounter a teaching that he will not understand (or that he may even find disagreeable or repelling!). For some, it may be the law on abstaining from alcohol; for others, it may be the requirement of parental consent for marriage; for still others, it may be the Bahá'í views on capital punishment. That law or principle may become a test for the believer and may even shake his faith.

When this occurs—or preferably before it occurs—we must keep in mind certain critical principles. One principle is intellectual humility. We must admit that we are not all-knowing. We do not have complete knowledge of the spiritual world. We have turned to God, through Bahá'u'lláh, because He does have this knowledge. We are Bahá'ís not simply because the Faith has good ideas or because its beliefs coincide with our own, but rather because through the religion of God, we can become spiritually educated. In order to become educated, one must first admit that he does not know, but desires to learn. With such an attitude, and with the help of prayer, study, reflection, and consulting with other Bahá'ís, we will eventually come to realize the wisdom of most laws and principles that we initially may not have understood.

This process of understanding, realizing the reasons underlying a Bahá'í Teaching, may take weeks, months, or even years. Bahá'u'lláh has given us an effective means to remain constant and steadfast while we are struggling to understand. He states that we must strive:

> to remain steadfast in the Cause of God . . . and to be unswerving in His love. And this can in no wise be attained except

50

through full recognition of Him; and full recognition cannot be obtained save by faith in the blessed words: 'He doeth whatsoever He willeth.' Whoso tenaciously cleaveth unto this sublime word and drinketh deep from the living waters of utterance which are inherent therein, will be imbued with such a constancy that all the books of the world will be powerless to deter him from the Mother Book.[156]

This principle ("He doeth whatsoever He willeth") implies that the Manifestations of God are infallible, that "whatever emanates from Them is identical with the truth, and conformable to reality. . . . Whatever They say is the word of God, and whatever They perform is an upright action. No believer has any right to criticize; his condition must be one of absolute submission, for the Manifestation arises with perfect wisdom. . . ."[157] Bahá'u'lláh says, "Whoso hath not recognized this sublime and fundamental verity, and hath failed to attain this most exalted station, the winds of doubt will agitate him, and the sayings of the infidels will distract his soul. He that hath acknowledged this principle will be endowed with the most perfect constancy."[158]

This principle does not mean that we are to accept blindly. Bahá'u'lláh teaches that we must first investigate the truth and recognize the Manifestation of God, ascertaining that He is the source of truth. Once we have done this, then we must carry out His laws and principles. Although we may not have been aware of it, probably all of us have throughout our lives believed in, and been carrying out, this principle of faithful obedience to an authority. For example, nearly all of us have been ill at some time in our lives. We visited a doctor who prescribed a remedy. We faithfully obeyed the instructions of the doctor by taking the prescribed medicine, and as a result, we recovered from the sickness. For all we know, the medicine that the doctor prescribed for us could have been poison! But because we had confidence in the doctor, because we had ascertained that he was a competent and able physician, we followed his instructions without question or hesitation. What then must be the response of those of us who have recognized Bahá'u'lláh, the Divine Physician?

Quotations for Reflection

1. Why should we obey the commandments of God?

"'Observe My commandments, for the love of My beauty.'"

(Bahá'u'lláh, *Kitáb-i-Aqdas*, parag. 4)

"O Son of Man! Neglect not My commandments if thou lovest My beauty, and forget not My counsels if thou wouldst attain My good pleasure." (Bahá'u'lláh, *Hidden Words*, Arabic #39)

2. What is the purpose of the one true God in manifesting Himself?

"The purpose of the one true God in manifesting Himself is to summon all mankind to truthfulness and sincerity, to piety and trustworthiness, to resignation and submissiveness to the Will of God, to forbearance and kindliness, to uprightness and wisdom. His object is to array every man with the mantle of a saintly character, and to adorn him with the ornament of holy and goodly deeds."

(*Gleanings from the Writings of Bahá'u'lláh*, p. 299)

3. What will be the effects of our obedience to the laws and principles of God?

"... whatsoever hath been set forth in the Book by the Pen of Glory is an effective means for the purging, the purification and sanctification of the souls of men and a source of prosperity and blessing."

(Bahá'u'lláh, *Ḥuqúqu'lláh* #40)

"You should rest assured that your strict adherence to the laws and observances enjoined by Bahá'u'lláh is the one power that can effectively guide and enable you to overcome the tests and trials of your life, and help you to continually grow and develop spiritually."

(On behalf of Shoghi Effendi, *Spiritual Foundations* #48)

"... acquisition of spiritual and moral character ... is the outcome of obedience to the divine laws and principles."

(Universal House of Justice, Riḍván 150 (1993), to the Bahá'ís of the World)

4. What are the blessings connected with the *Kitáb-i-Aqdas*?

"'This Book is a heaven which We have adorned with the stars of Our commandments and prohibitions.' 'Blessed the man who will read it, and ponder the verses sent down in it by God, the Lord of Power, the Almighty.' . . . 'Blessed the palate that savoreth its sweetness, and the perceiving eye that recognizeth that which is treasured therein, and the understanding heart that comprehendeth its allusions and mysteries.'... 'In such a manner hath the Kitáb-i-Aqdas been revealed that it attracteth and embraceth all the divinely appointed Dispensations. Blessed those who peruse it! Blessed those who apprehend it! Blessed those who meditate upon it! Blessed those who ponder its meaning! So vast is its range that it hath encompassed all men ere their recognition of it. Erelong will its sovereign power, its pervasive influence and the greatness of its might be manifested on earth.'"

(Bahá'u'lláh, quoted in *God Passes By*, p. 216)

5. The laws revealed by Bahá'u'lláh in the *Kitáb-i-Aqdas* serve what manifold purposes?

"Through His Law, Bahá'u'lláh gradually unveils the significance of the new levels of knowledge and behavior to which the peoples of the world are being called. He embeds His precepts in a setting of spiritual commentary, keeping ever before the mind of the reader the principle that these laws, no matter the subject with which they deal, serve the manifold purposes of bringing tranquillity to human society, raising the standard of human behavior, increasing the range of human understanding, and spiritualizing the life of each and all."

(Universal House of Justice, *Kitáb-i-Aqdas*, Introduction, p. 2)

6. What is the significance of the fasting period?

"It is essentially a period of meditation and prayer, of spiritual recuperation, during which the believer must strive to make the necessary readjustments in his inner life, and to refresh and reinvigorate the spiritual forces latent in his soul. Its significance and purpose are, therefore, fundamentally spiritual in character. Fasting is symbolic, and a reminder of abstinence from selfish and carnal desires."

(On behalf of Shoghi Effendi, *Lights of Guidance*, p. 233)

7. The practice of backbiting is condemned in what terms in the Bahá'í Writings?

"Ye have been forbidden to commit murder or adultery, or to engage in backbiting or calumny; shun ye, then, what hath been prohibited in the holy Books and Tablets."

(Bahá'u'lláh, *Kitáb-i-Aqdas*, parag. 19)

"As regards backbiting, i.e. discussing the faults of others in their absence, the teachings are very emphatic. In a Tablet to an American friend the Master wrote: 'The worst human quality and the most great sin is backbiting, more especially when it emanates from the tongues of the believers of God. If some means were devised so that the doors of backbiting were shut eternally and each one of the believers unsealed his lips in praise of others, then the Teachings of His Holiness Bahá'u'lláh would spread, the hearts be illumined, the spirits glorified, and the human world would attain to everlasting felicity.' . . . Bahá'u'lláh says in Hidden Words: 'Breathe not the sins of others so long as thou art a sinner. Shouldst thou transgress this command ACCURSED ART THOU.' The condemnation of backbiting could hardly be couched in stronger language than in these passages, and it is obviously one of the foremost obligations for Bahá'ís to set their faces against this practice. Even if what is said against another person be true, the mentioning of his faults to others still comes under the category of backbiting, and is forbidden."   (On behalf of Shoghi Effendi, *Lights of Guidance*, p. 88)

Illustration

"We had learned that to be with 'Abdu'l-Bahá was all life, joy and blessedness. We were to learn also that His Presence is a purifying fire. The pilgrimage to the Holy City is naught but a crucible in which the souls are tried; where the gold is purified and the dross is consumed. It did not seem possible that anything but love could ever again animate our words and actions. Yet that very afternoon, in my room with two of the believers, I spoke against a brother in the truth, finding fault with him, and giving vent to the evil in my own heart by my words. While we were still sitting together our Master who had been visiting the poor and sick, returned, and immediately sent for my spiritual mother, Lua, who was with us. He told her that during His absence one of His servants had spoken unkindly of another, and that it grieved His heart that the believers should not love one another or that they should speak against any soul. Then He charged her not to speak of it but to pray. A little later we all went to supper, and my hard heart was unconscious of its error, until, as my eyes sought the beloved face of my Master, I met His gaze, so full of gentleness and compassion that I was smitten to the heart. For in some marvellous way His eyes spoke to me; in that pure and perfect mirror I saw my wretched self and burst into tears. He took no notice of me for a while and everyone kindly continued with the supper while I sat in His dear Presence washing away some of my sins in tears. After a few moments He turned and smiled on me and spoke my name several times as though He were calling me to Him. In an instant such sweet happiness pervaded my soul, my heart was comforted with such infinite hope, that I knew He would cleanse me of all my sins."

(May Maxwell, *An Early Pilgrimage*, pp. 25-26)

Study References

1. See the *Kitáb-i-Aqdas* for discussion of the laws mentioned above and others. The "Synopsis and Codification," which is included after the text of the *Kitáb-i-Aqdas*, gives an outline and overview of all the laws of the *Kitáb-i-Aqdas*; it is an excellent tool in studying the Most Holy Book.

2. For guidance on which laws of the *Kitáb-i-Aqdas* are binding upon Bahá'ís in the West, see *Messages from the Universal House of Justice: 1963-1986*, pp. 277-79. Since the issuance of the guidance in *Messages*, the law of Ḥuqúqu'lláh has also become binding.

3. The book *Tablets of Bahá'u'lláh* contains many of the principles which lie at the very core of the Faith. 'Abdu'l-Bahá expounded, during the course of His journeys in America and Europe, the basic and distinguishing principles of His Father's Faith. Two sources containing His talks in the West are *The Promulgation of Universal Peace* and *Paris Talks*.

4. See Appendix F for a listing and explanation of the Bahá'í holy days.

Ḥuqúqu'lláh
and the Bahá'í Funds

"Indeed there lie concealed in this command, mysteries and benefits
which are beyond the comprehension of anyone save God,
the All-Knowing, the All-Informed."[159]
—Bahá'u'lláh

Bahá'u'lláh has declared that "the progress and promotion of the Cause of God depend on material means."[160] However, only Bahá'ís have the privilege of making material offerings to the Faith. The Bahá'í Faith does not solicit, or accept, offerings from those who are not followers of Bahá'u'lláh. Because only Bahá'ís can contribute towards the progress and promotion of God's Cause, giving materially to the Faith is a most significant spiritual obligation.

Another distinguishing feature of material offerings in the Faith is that the process of contribution must be characterized by dignity. Bahá'u'lláh has written, "At all times one must have the utmost regard for the dignity and honor of the Cause of God."[161] The Writings say that solicitation of individual believers is forbidden; only general appeals to the community of the believers are allowed. Material offerings are not to be enforced with pressure or intimidation. Rather, they are viewed as a spiritual duty that the individual fulfills out of love for the Faith of God. Each Bahá'í must therefore educate himself about these material offerings because they are as important as the other spiritual practices of the Bahá'í life. Moreover, they are a source of great spiritual and material blessings.

In the Faith, material offerings take two forms: Ḥuqúqu'lláh and the Bahá'í Funds. Ḥuqúqu'lláh (roughly pronounced "Ho-goog-o-la"), which means "the Right of God," is a law. Contributing to the Bahá'í Funds is a moral responsibility, although it does not rise to the level of a law. The significance and details of each are discussed below.

Ḥuqúqu'lláh (The Right of God)

The law of Ḥuqúqu'lláh is "the offering of a fixed portion of the value of the believer's possessions."[162] "Should anyone acquire one hundred mithqáls† of gold, nineteen mithqáls thereof are God's and to be rendered unto Him, the Fashioner of earth and heaven."[163] Is God in need of our material goods? 'Abdu'l-Bahá has explained that "God verily is the All-Possessing, exalted above the need of any gift from His creatures."[164] However, in His bounty, God has given us the privilege of materially contributing to the progress of His Faith by returning unto Him that which is His "Right." "In this glorious Dispensation the treasures laid up by kings and queens are not worthy of mention, nor will they be acceptable in the presence of God. However, a grain of mustard offered by His loved ones will be extolled in the exalted court of His holiness and invested with the ornament of His acceptance."[165]

Bahá'u'lláh refers to the law of Ḥuqúqu'lláh as ranking in importance immediately after the two great obligations of recognizing God and being steadfast in His Cause.[166] In addition to promoting the activities of the Faith, this law creates a direct link between the individual believer and the Central Institution of the Faith because the Universal House of Justice is the recipient of the Right of God. Furthermore, through the law, believers directly promote a spiritual solution to the economic problems of the world. This is a means for "the elimination of extremes of wealth and poverty" and for the bringing about of "a more equitable distribution of resources."[167] It is a "sacred law which enables each one to express his or her personal sense of devotion to God in a profoundly private act of conscience that promotes the common good."[168]

The Bahá'í Writings describe the numerous blessings of obedience

---

†A "mithqál" is a unit of weight. See Appendix E for details.

to this law: Ḥuqúqu'lláh "enables the friends to recognize the elevation of their economic activity to the level of divine acceptability, it is a means for the purification of their wealth and a magnet attracting divine blessings."[169] "It is clear and evident that the payment of the Right of God is conducive to prosperity, to blessing, and to honor and divine protection."[170] Further, "it is the source of grace, abundance, and of all good. It is a bounty which shall remain with every soul in every world of the worlds of God,"[171] and its results "will last as long as the kingdom of earth and heaven will endure."[172]

In the sight of God, Ḥuqúqu'lláh is acceptable only if offered in the right spirit: "And such benefits will indeed accrue if the Ḥuqúq is offered with the utmost joy and radiance and in a spirit of perfect humility and lowliness."[173] Acquiescence, resignation, willing submission, and eagerness are among other qualities the believer should strive for in making the offering. Therefore, obeying the law is not simply a matter of writing a check, but involves spiritual attitudes and qualities.†

As obedience to this law brings blessings, negligence or failure to offer God His Right causes one to be deprived of these bounties: "Deal not faithlessly with the Right of God. . . . He who dealeth faithlessly with God shall in justice meet with faithlessness himself. . . ."[174] Accordingly, Ḥuqúqu'lláh is a "unique test"[175] for the believers, enabling us to become "firm and steadfast in faith and certitude."[176]

The Bahá'í Funds

The second form of material offerings in the Faith is contribution to the Bahá'í Funds. Support of the Bahá'í Funds is "an integral part of the Bahá'í way of life."[177] When a person becomes a Bahá'í, he becomes a coworker in the Faith of God. He has the bounty of devoting his material possessions, no matter how limited, to the work of the Faith. Those who have not accepted Bahá'u'lláh do not have this spiritual privilege.

The Universal House of Justice has explained, "Contributing to the Fund is a service that every believer can render, be he poor or wealthy; for this is a spiritual responsibility in which the amount given is not

---

†Guidelines for computation of Ḥuqúqu'lláh are discussed in detail in Appendix E.

important. It is the degree of the sacrifice of the giver, the love with which he makes his gift, and the unity of all the friends in this service which bring spiritual confirmations."[178]

The major Bahá'í Funds to which believers are encouraged to contribute are the Local, National, Continental, and International Funds. In areas where there exists a Local Spiritual Assembly, the Assembly will have a Fund to support the activities of the Bahá'ís in that locality. Similarly, each National Spiritual Assembly has a Fund which is expended for activities in its country. Likewise, Continental and International institutions of the Faith administer activities through the use of Funds contributed to them by the believers.

Consistency and confidentiality are two aspects of contributing to the Funds. Consistency in contributions is important in order that the institutions of the Faith may effectively make and carry out plans. Second, contributions are confidential. Only the contributor and the receiving institution know who has contributed and how much has been given.

A special purpose fund existing at the present time that is of great importance is the Arc Projects Fund. During these concluding years of the century, a vast project is underway in the Holy Land, in Haifa, Israel, involving the construction of the Terraces of the Shrine of the Báb and the buildings of the World Administrative Center of the Faith. These buildings, which together form a semicircular "arc," are being built on Mt. Carmel, described by the prophet Isaiah three thousand years ago. Isaiah at that time announced that "it shall come to pass in the last days, that the mountain of the Lord's house shall be established in the top of the mountains, and shall be exalted above the hills; and all nations shall flow unto it."[179] We are now witnessing the fulfillment of this prophecy through the Arc Projects.

The Universal House of Justice has explained that these projects are of "profound significance."[180] They are much more than the erection of buildings to meet the expanding needs of the Bahá'í World Center. These projects are central to the work of the Faith in eliminating the root causes of the suffering now afflicting humanity.[181] At this time, the "two primary tasks" facing every follower of Bahá'u'lláh are "teaching the Faith to every thirsting soul," and "providing the material means for the completion of the monumental projects being pursued on Mount Carmel."[182]

Comparison of Ḥuqúqu'lláh and the Bahá'í Funds

There exist a number of differences between Ḥuqúqu'lláh and the Bahá'í Funds. First, the payment of Ḥuqúqu'lláh has priority over all other offerings: In paying Ḥuqúqu'lláh, we are not donating our own money to the Faith, but are returning to God that which is His "Right." Second, offering Ḥuqúqu'lláh is a law, while contributing to the Fund is not obligatory, although it is a moral responsibility. Third, Ḥuqúqu'lláh is determined precisely through the use of specific guidelines; whereas, there are no rules related to the amount a Bahá'í should contribute to the Fund. Lastly, the disposal of Ḥuqúqu'lláh is left to the Central Authority of the Faith, the Universal House of Justice; the disposal of the other Funds is carried out by the institution to which they are contributed.

Ḥuqúqu'lláh and the Fund are similar, however, in that the dignity and purity of the Faith must be maintained at all times in relation to these obligations. No compulsion or psychological pressure should be brought upon Bahá'ís to make their offerings. The friends must act voluntarily out of their love for Bahá'u'lláh.

Quotations for Reflection

1. What is the law of Ḥuqúqu'lláh?

"Should anyone acquire one hundred mithqáls of gold, nineteen mithqáls thereof are God's and to be rendered unto Him, the Fashioner of earth and heaven. Take heed, O people, lest ye deprive yourselves of so great a bounty. This We have commanded you, though We are well able to dispense with you and with all who are in the heavens and on earth; in it there are benefits and wisdoms beyond the ken of anyone but God, the Omniscient, the All-Informed."

(Bahá'u'lláh, *Kitáb-i-Aqdas*, parag. 97)

2. What are the blessings resulting from obedience to the law of Ḥuqúqu'lláh?

"Say: By this means He hath desired to purify what ye possess and to enable you to draw nigh unto such stations as none can comprehend save those whom God hath willed. He, in truth, is the Beneficent, the Gracious, the Bountiful. . . . He, verily, hath willed for you that which is yet beyond your knowledge, but which shall be known to you when, after this fleeting life, your souls soar heavenwards and the trappings of your earthly joys are folded up. Thus admonisheth you He in Whose possession is the Guarded Tablet."

(Bahá'u'lláh, *Kitáb-i-Aqdas*, parag. 97)

"Those who have observed this weighty ordinance have received heavenly blessings and in both worlds their faces have shone radiantly and their nostrils have been perfumed by the sweet savors of God's tender mercy. One of the tokens of His consummate wisdom is that the payment of the Ḥuqúq will enable the donors to become firm and steadfast and will exert a great influence on their hearts and souls. Furthermore the Ḥuqúq will be used for charitable purposes."

('Abdu'l-Bahá, *Ḥuqúqu'lláh* #62)

3. In what spirit should Ḥuqúqu'lláh be offered?

"Were a person to offer all the treasures of the earth at the cost of debasing the honor of the Cause of God, were it even less than a grain of mustard, such an offering would not be permissible. All the world hath belonged and will always belong to God. If one spontaneously offereth Ḥuqúq with the utmost joy and radiance it will be acceptable, and not otherwise."   (Bahá'u'lláh, *Ḥuqúqu'lláh* #27)

4. Is anyone besides Bahá'ís allowed to contribute to the Bahá'í Fund?

"One of the distinguishing features of the Cause of God is its principle of nonacceptance of financial contributions for its own purposes from non-Bahá'ís: support of the Bahá'í Fund is a bounty reserved by Bahá'u'lláh to His declared followers. This bounty imposes full responsibility for financial support of the Faith on the believers alone, every one of whom is called upon to do his utmost to ensure that the constant and liberal outpouring of means is maintained and increased to meet the growing needs of the Cause."

(Universal House of Justice, *Lights of Guidance*, pp. 250-51)

5. Are only wealthy believers responsible for contributing to the Fund?

"Every Bahá'í, no matter how poor, must realize what a grave responsibility he has to shoulder in this connection, and should have confidence that his spiritual progress as a believer in the World Order of Bahá'u'lláh will largely depend upon the measure in which he proves, in deeds, his readiness to support materially the Divine institutions of His Faith."   (On behalf of Shoghi Effendi, *Bahá'í Funds* #20)

6. Is it the amount of the contribution to the Fund which is important?

"The overwhelming majority of the Bahá'ís in the world are poor people, but it is to the believers, and to the believers alone, that Bahá'u'lláh has given the bounty of contributing the material things of this world for the progress of His Faith. It is not the amount of the contribution which is important, but the degree of self-sacrifice that it entails—for it is this that attracts the confirmations of God."
                    (Universal House of Justice, *Lights of Guidance*, p. 250)

7. Why is it important to contribute to the Arc Projects Fund? Would it not be a better use of money to try to relieve the distress and suffering of mankind by feeding the hungry, helping the poor, etc.?

"The call for contributions to the Arc Projects Fund, far from being a diversion of resources which might otherwise be used to help relieve the distress of mankind, offers the followers of Bahá'u'lláh a providential opportunity to participate in an endeavor which is central to the work of the Faith in eradicating the causes of the appalling suffering now afflicting humanity.

"The Bahá'í community encourages and supports the manifold efforts being made by people of goodwill to better the condition of humankind and promote unity and harmony among the peoples and nations of the earth. However, the believers should never, for even one moment, lose sight of the fact that the crisis now engulfing every part of the planet is essentially spiritual. 'That which the Lord hath ordained as the sovereign remedy and mightiest instrument for the healing of all the world', Bahá'u'lláh emphatically states, 'is the union of all its peoples in one universal Cause, one common Faith.' Our acute awareness of the magnitude of the misery which so many groups and individuals are experiencing should spur us on to ever-greater exertions, inspired and animated by an abiding consciousness that only through the World Order of Bahá'u'lláh can the multitudinous problems burdening humanity be resolved."

(Universal House of Justice, January 4, 1994, to all National Assemblies)

Illustration

"The Bahá'í friends [in a village in the Pacific region] . . . in their love for Bahá'u'lláh and the Universal House of Justice, wanted to contribute to the Arc Fund, but there was no cash in the village. They decided to contribute taroes—a root crop—to the Arc Fund. Each family contributed taroes until there were 21 filled bags. Then the youth of the village carried the taro bags over mountainous bush tracks, a full two days walk, until they reached the road where trucks were going to the main town. They sold the taroes in the capital city and raised 110.00 Kina (U.S. $83.00). They gave the money . . . to the National Spiritual Assembly for the Arc Fund, National Centre Fund and National Fund. This is a large and sacrificial sum for these people and for their village."

("Vineyard of the Lord," March 1996)

Study References

1. For more on the law of Ḥuqúqu'lláh, see the compilation entitled *Ḥuqúqu'lláh* and the booklet *Ḥuqúqu'lláh: A Study Guide.*

2. For details on the calculation of *Ḥuqúqu'lláh*, see Appendix E.

3. For more on the Bahá'í Funds, see the compilation *Lifeblood of the Cause: Bahá'í Funds and Contributions.*

4. For more on the Arc Projects, see *A Wider Horizon*, pp. 50-54, 221-26.

Service

*"Arise ye, under all conditions, to render service to the Cause,
for God will assuredly assist you through the power of His sovereignty
which overshadoweth the worlds."*[183]
—Bahá'u'lláh

The Spiritual Duty of Service

Many of the sacred duties of the Bahá'í life, such as prayer and meditation, are very personal, being performed in the privacy of one's home. However, we should not conclude from this that in order for us to develop spiritually, we must withdraw from society, like the monks of past ages. To the contrary, spiritual progress requires that we interact with other people. The spiritual powers generated by the practices of prayer, meditation, and study must be converted into service to humanity. The effects of worship are not significant or lasting, unless worship is translated into service.[184] Bahá'u'lláh states, "That one indeed is a man who, today, dedicateth himself to the service of the entire human race. The Great Being saith: Blessed and happy is he that ariseth to promote the best interests of the peoples and kindreds of the earth."[185] Therefore, service is central to our spiritual growth.

Service takes many forms. One of its forms is service to humanity generally: "Think ye at all times of rendering some service to every member of the human race. Pay ye no heed to aversion and rejection, to disdain, hostility, injustice: act ye in the opposite way. Be ye sincerely kind, not in appearance only. Let each one of God's loved ones centre his attention on this: to be the Lord's mercy to man; to be the Lord's grace. Let him do some good to every person whose path he crosseth, and be of some benefit to him. Let him improve the character of each and all, and reorient the minds of men."[186]

In striving to be of service to others, one may reflect on such questions as: How can I serve my family members? How can I be of service to those I meet at school or work or in my neighborhood? Can I visit the sick or assist the elderly? It may be easy to serve those I love, but how can I be of service to those who seem unlovable? How can I apply the Bahá'í principles in solving the current problems of society and thereby serve humanity? How can I purify my motives so that I am not serving for praise or recognition, but simply out of love for my fellowman and in obedience to God?

Service also takes the form of the selfless pursuit of one's trade or profession: "O people of Bahá! It is incumbent upon each one of you to engage in some occupation—such as a craft, a trade or the like."[187] He who strives for excellence in his work and carries out his duties in a spirit of service to others is, in the sight of God, engaging in worship. 'Abdu'l-Bahá has said, "The man who makes a piece of notepaper to the best of his ability, conscientiously, concentrating all his forces on perfecting it, is giving praise to God. Briefly, all effort and exertion put forth by man from the fullness of his heart is worship, if it is prompted by the highest motives and the will to do service to humanity."[188] Even young Bahá'ís, who have not yet begun their life's work, should think of their studies and of their training for a trade or profession as part of a lifetime of service: "It is the obligation of a Bahá'í to educate his children; likewise it is the duty of the children to acquire knowledge of the arts and sciences and to learn a trade or a profession whereby they, in turn, can earn their living and support their families. This, for a Bahá'í youth, is in itself a service to God. . . ."[189]

In addition to maintaining a general attitude of service towards others, we, as Bahá'ís, have the added privilege and blessing of serving humanity through service to the Faith of God: "How great the blessedness that awaiteth him that hath attained the honor of serving the Almighty!"[190] Perhaps the most important form of service to the Faith is teaching, which was discussed in a previous chapter. In addition to teaching, the individual Bahá'í may serve in any way that will promote the progress of the Cause of God. For example, a believer serves by supporting the goals and projects of the Local Spiritual Assembly, by teaching children's classes, by hosting Feast, or by serving on an Assembly or committee.

Two principles are relevant here. First, the individual must be enterprising, must be willing to take initiative to be of service to the Faith and to other Bahá'ís; he should not wait to be asked to participate. Second, the believer should seek out the guidance of Bahá'í institutions—for example, the Local Spiritual Assembly—to learn what are the needs of the Faith. Spiritual Assemblies are able to guide the believers in selecting paths of service that will be most beneficial.

We must come to see service as a part of all aspects of the Bahá'í life. This attitude was exemplified by 'Abdu'l-Bahá whose life is a perfect model of what it means to serve others. 'Abdu'l-Bahá saw Himself as a servant: "My station is the station of servitude—a servitude which is complete, pure and real, firmly established, enduring, obvious, explicitly revealed and subject to no interpretation whatever. . . ."[191] In Arabic, the title "'Abdu'l-Bahá" means servant of Bahá. He Himself said, "No name, no title, no mention, no commendation have I, nor will ever have, except 'Abdu'l-Bahá. This is my longing. This is my greatest yearning. This is my eternal life. This is my everlasting glory."[192] He did attain this longing as His whole life was dedicated to service to the Faith and to humanity. We, as Bahá'ís, must strive to follow His example, for "Service to humanity is service to God."[193]

Community Involvement

One of the most important ways an individual can be of service is by promoting love and unity within the Bahá'í community. This may be done by living the Bahá'í life, by being of service to other Bahá'ís, and by refraining from backbiting and negative criticism. We also serve to strengthen the community through our active participation in Bahá'í community life. Among the most significant features of community life are involvement in the Nineteen Day Feast, Bahá'í elections, and consultation.

1. Nineteen Day Feast

The Nineteen Day Feast, which gathers once every nineteen days, is an institution of which all Bahá'ís are members. "It is intended to promote unity, ensure progress, and foster joy."[194] 'Abdu'l-Bahá has written, "Give ye great weight to the Nineteen Day gatherings, so that on these occasions the beloved of the Lord and the handmaids of the Merciful may turn their faces toward the Kingdom, chant the communes, beseech God's help, become joyfully enamored each of the other, and grow in purity and holiness, and in the fear of God, and in resistance to passion and self. Thus will they separate themselves from this elemental world, and immerse themselves in the ardors of the spirit."[195] Moreover, the Writings indicate that Feast "is the key to affection and fellowship. It diffuseth the oneness of mankind."[196]

The Feast has three distinct but related portions: the devotional, the administrative, and the social parts. During the devotional portion, prayers and passages from the holy texts are recited. During the administrative part, the Local Spiritual Assembly reports its plans and activities to the community and shares news and messages. The community discusses its affairs and the progress of the Faith. The Assembly also receives the thoughts, recommendations, and constructive criticism of the believers through a process called consultation (discussed below). The third part of the Feast is the social portion, during which the friends partake of refreshments and engage in fellowship. The Feast is usually held on the first day of each Bahá'í month.†

"Attendance at Nineteen Day Feasts is not obligatory but very important, and every believer should consider it a duty and privilege to be present on such occasions."[197] With what attitude should we enter the Feast? "But when you present yourselves in the meetings, before entering them, free yourselves from all that you have in your heart, free your thoughts and your minds from all else save God, and speak to your heart. . . . Each one of you must think how to make happy and pleased the other members of your Assembly, and each one must consider all those who are present as better and greater than himself, and each one must consider himself less than the rest. Know their station as high, and think of your own station as low. Should you act and live according to these behests, know verily, of a certainty, that that Feast is the Heavenly Food. That Supper is the 'Lord's Supper'!"[198] "If this feast be held in the proper fashion, the friends will, once in nineteen days, find themselves spiritually restored, and endued with a power that is not of this world."[199]

---

†Appendix F provides a listing of the dates of the Nineteen Day Feast.

2. Bahá'í Elections

In addition to taking part in Feast, the individual Bahá'í is connected to the community through Bahá'í elections. In every town or city where nine or more adult Bahá'ís reside, a Local Spiritual Assembly must be elected. All Bahá'ís 21 years of age or older are eligible to vote and to be elected. Bahá'í elections differ completely from modern-day political elections. They are characterized by spirituality, purity, dignity, and unity. Nomination of candidates, electioneering, and campaigning are strictly forbidden in Bahá'í elections. Thus, Bahá'ís have the absolute and complete freedom to vote for those whom they feel are most qualified. Each Bahá'í must consult his conscience and vote for those "who can best combine the necessary qualities of unquestioned loyalty, of selfless devotion, of a well-trained mind, of recognized ability and mature experience."[200] Voting is carried out in an atmosphere of prayer, meditation, selflessness, and detachment. Elections for the Local Spiritual Assembly take place once a year on April 21st, the anniversary of the Declaration of Bahá'u'lláh.

Another election in which Bahá'ís take part is that which is held at District Convention. At this convention, the Bahá'ís in a district, which usually encompasses a number of towns and cities, elect one or more delegates who will represent that district at National Convention. These delegates will vote for the National Spiritual Assembly of the Bahá'ís of the country. Additionally, the delegates take part in consultations on the national level. Both the District and National Conventions are held once each year.

3. Consultation

A spiritual process that is critical to many aspects of Bahá'í community life is consultation. Bahá'u'lláh exhorts Baha'ís to take counsel together in all matters. Consultation is used during Feast, by Assemblies and committees, at Convention, within families, and among individuals. Consultation is a method of decision-making, which has as its purpose the finding of a solution to a problem.[201] Those consulting must listen open-mindedly to the views of others and share their own views: "The shining spark of truth cometh forth only after the clash of differing opinions."[202]

Consultation, however, is not merely a discussion or the voicing of personal opinions; it is "spiritual conference."[203] The individuals consulting must fulfil certain spiritual prerequisites before consultation will be successful. The "first condition is absolute love and harmony amongst the members of the assembly." The "second condition" is that they "must when coming together turn their faces to the Kingdom on High and ask aid from the Realm of Glory."[204]

Further, those who consult must proceed "with the utmost devotion, courtesy, dignity, care and moderation to express their views. They must in every matter search out the truth and not insist upon their own opinion, for stubbornness and persistence in one's views will lead ultimately to discord and wrangling and the truth will remain hidden."[205] The goal is to achieve unanimity in the decision: "If after discussion, a decision be carried unanimously, well and good; but if, the Lord forbid, differences of opinion should arise, a majority of voices must prevail."[206]

Once a decision is reached unanimously or by majority vote, *all* must fully and wholeheartedly support and carry out the decision, even those who may have voted against the idea. "If they agree upon a subject, even though it be wrong, it is better than to disagree and be in the right, for this difference will produce the demolition of the divine foundation. Though one of the parties may be in the right and they disagree that will be the cause of a thousand wrongs, but if they agree and both parties are in the wrong, as it is in unity the truth will be revealed and the wrong made right."[207] Consultation is a powerful and practical tool that Bahá'ís can use in all aspects of their lives: "Take ye counsel together in all matters, inasmuch as consultation is the lamp of guidance which leadeth the way, and is the bestower of understanding."[208]

Quotations for Reflection

1. What is the spiritual significance of service?

"Again, is there any deed in the world that would be nobler than service to the common good? Is there any greater blessing conceivable for a man, than that he should become the cause of the education, the development, the prosperity and honor of his fellow-creatures? No, by the Lord God! The highest righteousness of all is for blessed souls to

70

take hold of the hands of the helpless and deliver them out of their ignorance and abasement and poverty, and with pure motives, and only for the sake of God, to arise and energetically devote themselves to the service of the masses, forgetting their own worldly advantage and working only to serve the general good. . . . 'The best of men are those who serve the people; the worst of men are those who harm the people.'"

(Abdu'l-Bahá, *The Secret of Divine Civilization*, p. 103)

"There is nothing that brings success in the Faith like service. Service is the magnet which draws the divine confirmations. Thus, when a person is active, they are blessed by the Holy Spirit. When they are inactive, the Holy Spirit cannot find a repository in their being, and thus they are deprived of its healing and quickening rays."

(On behalf of Shoghi Effendi, *Living the Life*, p. 34)

2. Will we be assisted if we arise to serve God's Faith?

"Arise to further My Cause, and to exalt My Word amongst men. We are with you at all times, and shall strengthen you through the power of truth. We are truly almighty. Whoso hath recognized Me will arise and serve Me with such determination that the powers of earth and heaven shall be unable to defeat his purpose."

(Bahá'u'lláh, *Kitáb-i-Aqdas*, parag. 38)

"Should any one arise for the triumph of our Cause, him will God render victorious though tens of thousands of enemies be leagued against him. And if his love for Me wax stronger, God will establish his ascendancy over all the powers of earth and heaven."

(Bahá'u'lláh, quoted in *The World Order of Bahá'u'lláh*, p. 106)

3. How can we be occupied with our trade or profession and, at the same time, serve the Faith?

"The advice that Shoghi Effendi gave you regarding the division of your time between serving the Cause and attending to your other duties was also given to many other friends both by Bahá'u'lláh and the Master. It is a compromise between the two verses of the Aqdas, one making it incumbent upon every Bahá'í to serve the promotion of the

Faith and the other that every soul should be occupied in some form of occupation that will benefit society. In one of His Tablets Bahá'u'lláh says that the highest form of detachment in this day is to be occupied with some profession and be self-supporting. A good Bahá'í, therefore, is the one who so arranges his life as to devote time both to his material needs and also to the service of the Cause."

(On behalf of Shoghi Effendi, *Living the Life*, pp. 12-13)

4. In order to live the Teachings of the Faith, is it necessary to be active with the Bahá'í community?

"To live the Teachings of the Cause should be the paramount concern of every true believer, and the only way to do so is to commune both in spirit and through actual concrete means with the entire community of the faithful. The Bahá'í Cause encourages community life and makes it a duty for every one of its followers to become a living, a fully active and responsible member of the worldwide Bahá'í fellowship." (On behalf of Shoghi Effendi, *Lights of Guidance*, pp. 475-76)

5. What is the significance of the Nineteen Day Feast?

"This festivity, which is held on a day of the nineteen-day month, was established by His Holiness the Báb, and the Blessed Beauty [Bahá'u'lláh] directed, confirmed and warmly encouraged the holding of it. It is, therefore, of the utmost importance. You should unquestionably see to it with the greatest care, and make its value known, so that it may become solidly established on a permanent basis. Let the beloved of God gather together and associate most lovingly and spiritually and happily with one another, conducting themselves with the greatest courtesy and self-restraint. Let them read the holy verses, as well as essays which are of benefit, and the letters of 'Abdu'l-Bahá; encourage and inspire one another to love each and all; chant the prayers with serenity and joy; give eloquent talks, and praise the matchless Lord.

"The host, with complete self-effacement, showing kindness to all, must be a comfort to each one, and serve the friends with his own hands.

"If the Feast is befittingly held, in the manner described, then this supper will verily be the Lord's Supper, for its fruits will be the very fruits of that Supper, and its influence the same."

('Abdu'l-Bahá, Stirring of the Spirit #2)

6. In Bahá'í elections, who should be elected?

"Due regard must be paid to their actual capacity and present attainments, and only those who are best qualified for membership, be they men or women, and irrespective of social standing, should be elected to the extremely responsible position of a member of the Bahá'í Assembly."

(Shoghi Effendi, Bahá'í Elections #7)

"They should disregard personalities and concentrate their attention on the qualities and requirements of office, without prejudice, passion or partiality. The Assembly should be representative of the choicest and most varied and capable elements in every Bahá'í community. . . ."

(Shoghi Effendi, Bahá'í Elections #11)

7. What are the prime requisites for those who consult?

"The prime requisites for them that take counsel together are purity of motive, radiance of spirit, detachment from all else save God, attraction to His Divine Fragrances, humility and lowliness amongst His loved ones, patience and long-suffering in difficulties and servitude to His exalted Threshold. Should they be graciously aided to acquire these attributes, victory from the unseen Kingdom of Bahá shall be vouchsafed to them. . . . The members thereof must take counsel together in such wise that no occasion for ill-feeling or discord may arise. This can be attained when every member expresseth with absolute freedom his own opinion and setteth forth his argument. Should any one oppose, he must on no account feel hurt for not until matters are fully discussed can the right way be revealed. The shining spark of truth cometh forth only after the clash of differing opinions."

('Abdu'l-Bahá, Consultation #9)

Illustration

"One day when Lua Getsinger was in 'Akká to see the Master, He said to her, that He was too busy today to call upon a friend of His who was very ill and poor and He wished her to go in His place. Take him food and care for him as I have been doing, He concluded. He told her where this man was to be found and she went gladly, proud that 'Abdu'l-Bahá should trust her with this mission.

"She returned quickly. 'Master,' she exclaimed, 'surely you cannot realize to what a terrible place you sent me. I almost fainted from the awful stench, the filthy rooms, the degrading condition of that man and his house. I fled lest I contract some terrible disease.'

"Sadly and sternly 'Abdu'l-Bahá regarded her. 'Dost thou desire to serve God,' He said, 'serve thy fellow man for in him dost thou see the image and likeness of God.' He told her to go back to this man's house. If it is filthy she should clean it; if this brother of yours is dirty, bathe him; if he is hungry, feed him. Do not return until this is done. Many times had He done this for him and cannot she serve him once?"

(*Vignettes from the Life of 'Abdu'l-Bahá*, pp. 91-92)

Study References

1. For more on service, see the compilation entitled *Living the Life*.

2. For more on 'Abdu'l-Bahá's life of service, see *'Abdu'l-Bahá* by H. M. Balyuzi, a full-length biography, and Annamarie Honnold's *Vignettes from the Life of 'Abdu'l-Bahá*, which is a collection of anecdotes and stories about the life of 'Abdu'l-Bahá. *Maḥmúd's Diary* is a fascinating chronicle of 'Abdu'l-Bahá's journey in America.

3. For more on the Nineteen Day Feast, see the compilation entitled *Stirring of the Spirit: Celebrating the Institution of the Nineteen Day Feast*. For a listing of the dates of Nineteen Day Feast, see Appendix F.

4. For more on Bahá'í elections, see the compilation entitled *Bahá'í Elections*.

5. For more on consultation, see the compilation entitled *Consultation*.

Appendix A

The Obligatory Prayers

'Abdu'l-Bahá has written, "Know thou that in every word and movement of the obligatory prayer there are allusions, mysteries and a wisdom that man is unable to comprehend, and letters and scrolls cannot contain."[209] Because "every word and movement" has a profound significance, it is important for us to properly perform the Obligatory Prayers. The Guardian and the Universal House of Justice have given guidance about some of the features and movements of these prayers. Their statements have been included in this Appendix (in footnotes to the text of the prayers) to assist the reader to better understand how the prayers are performed.

In carrying out these movements, we should keep in mind that the "simplicity characterizing the offering of Bahá'í prayers, whether obligatory or otherwise, should be maintained. Rigidity and rituals should be strictly avoided."[210] Although we are free to share with others our interpretation of how to perform the Obligatory Prayers, we should not impose our understanding on others.

Instructions Related to All Three Obligatory Prayers

"The friends are free to choose any one of these three prayers, but have to follow the instructions revealed by Bahá'u'lláh concerning them."[211]

"The daily prayers are to be said each one for himself, aloud or silent makes no difference. There is no congregational prayer except that for the dead. We read healing and other prayers in our meetings, but the daily prayer is a personal obligation, so someone else reading it is not quite the same thing as saying it for yourself."[212]

"Question: The believers have been enjoined to face in the direction of the Qiblih when reciting their Obligatory Prayers; in what direction should they turn when offering other prayers and devotions?"

"Answer: Facing in the direction of the Qiblih is a fixed requirement for the recitation of obligatory prayer, but for other prayers and devotions one may follow what the merciful Lord hath revealed in the Qur'án: 'Whichever way ye turn, there is the face of God.'"[213]

Specific Instructions Related to Each Prayer

Short Obligatory Prayer[†]

(TO BE RECITED ONCE IN TWENTY-FOUR HOURS, AT NOON)[‡]

I bear witness, O my God, that Thou hast created me to know Thee and to worship Thee. I testify, at this moment, to my powerlessness and to Thy might, to my poverty and to Thy wealth.

There is none other God but Thee, the Help in Peril, the Self-Subsisting. *(Prayers and Meditations*, p. 314)

Medium Obligatory Prayer

(TO BE RECITED DAILY, IN THE MORNING, AT NOON, AND IN THE EVENING)[ʃ]

[†] "Question: Should the third Obligatory Prayer [i.e. the short Obligatory Prayer] be offered while seated or standing? Answer: It is preferable and more fitting to stand in an attitude of humble reverence." (Bahá'u'lláh, *Kitáb-i-Aqdas*, Q& A #81).

[‡] "The definition of 'noon' as the period 'from noon till sunset' applies to the recitation of the short Obligatory Prayer as well as the medium one." (*Kitáb-i-Aqdas*, Note #5).

[ʃ] "Regarding the definition of the words 'morning', 'noon' and 'evening', at which times the currently binding medium Obligatory Prayer is to be recited, Bahá'u'lláh has stated that these coincide with 'sunrise, noon and sunset' (Q&A #83). He specifies that the 'allowable times for Obligatory Prayers are from morning till noon, from noon till sunset, and from sunset till two hours thereafter'. Further, 'Abdu'l-Bahá has stated that the morning Obligatory Prayer may be said as early as dawn." (*Kitáb-i-Aqdas*, Note #5).

Whoso wisheth to pray, let him wash his hands,
and while he washeth, let him say:[†]

Strengthen my hand, O my God, that it may take hold of Thy Book with such steadfastness that the hosts of the world shall have no power over it. Guard it, then, from meddling with whatsoever doth not belong unto it. Thou art, verily, the Almighty, the Most Powerful.

And while washing his face, let him say:

I have turned my face unto Thee, O my Lord! Illumine it with the light of Thy countenance. Protect it, then, from turning to anyone but Thee.

Then let him stand up, and facing the Qiblih
(Point of Adoration, i.e., Bahjí, 'Akká), let him say:

God testifieth that there is none other God but Him. His are the kingdoms of Revelation and of creation. He, in truth, hath manifested Him Who is the Day-Spring of Revelation, Who conversed on Sinai, through Whom the Supreme Horizon hath been made to shine, and the Lote-Tree beyond which there is no passing hath spoken, and through Whom the call hath been proclaimed unto all who are in heaven and on earth: "Lo, the All-Possessing is come. Earth and heaven, glory and dominion are God's, the Lord of all men, and the Possessor of the Throne on high and of earth below!"

Let him, then, bend down, with hands resting on the knees, and say:

Exalted art Thou above my praise and the praise of anyone beside me, above my description and the description of all who are in heaven and all who are on earth!

---

† "The prescribed ablutions consist of washing the hands and the face in preparation for prayer. In the case of the medium Obligatory Prayer, this is accompanied by the recitation of certain verses." (*Kitáb-i-Aqdas*, Note #34) "Question: Are ablutions for the morning prayer still valid for the noonday prayer? And similarly, are ablutions carried out at noon still valid in the evening? Answer: Ablutions are connected with the Obligatory Payer for which they are performed, and must be renewed for each prayer." (Bahá'u'lláh, *Kitáb-i-Aqdas*, Q & A #66).

Then, standing with open hands,
palms upward toward the face, let him say:

Disappoint not, O my God, him that hath, with beseeching fingers, clung to the hem of Thy mercy and Thy grace, O Thou Who of those who show mercy art the Most Merciful!

Let him, then, be seated and say:†

I bear witness to Thy unity and Thy oneness, and that Thou art God, and that there is none other God beside Thee. Thou hast, verily, revealed Thy Cause, fulfilled Thy Covenant, and opened wide the door of Thy grace to all that dwell in heaven and on earth. Blessing and peace, salutation and glory, rest upon Thy loved ones, whom the changes and chances of the world have not deterred from turning unto Thee, and who have given their all, in the hope of obtaining that which is with Thee. Thou art, in truth, the Ever-Forgiving, the All-Bountiful.

If anyone choose to recite instead of the long verse these words: "God testifieth that there is none other God but Him, the Help in Peril, the Self-Subsisting," it would be sufficient. And likewise, it would suffice were he, while seated, to choose to recite these words: "I bear witness to Thy unity and Thy oneness, and that Thou art God, and that there is none other God beside Thee."

(*Prayers and Meditations*, pp. 314-16)

Long Obligatory Prayer

(To be Recited Once in Twenty-Four Hours)‡

---

† "... one of the believers asked the Guardian a question about the correct position for sitting. From the context it seems clear that this question is related to the medium Prayer, but this is not explicitly stated. The Guardian's reply states that sitting on a chair is permissible, but to sit on the floor is preferable and more fitting." (On behalf of the Universal House of Justice, *Lights of Guidance*, p. 467)

‡ "... it hath been ordained, 'one should perform it at whatever time one findeth oneself in a state of humbleness and longing adoration'. ..." (Bahá'u'lláh, *Kitáb-i-Aqdas*, Q&A #82).

Whoso wisheth to recite this prayer, let him stand up and turn unto God,
and, as he standeth in his place, let him gaze to the right and to the left,
as if awaiting the mercy of his Lord, the Most Merciful,
the Compassionate. Then let him say:

O Thou Who art the Lord of all names and the Maker of the heavens! I beseech Thee by them Who are the Day-Springs of Thine invisible Essence, the Most Exalted, the All-Glorious, to make of my prayer a fire that will burn away the veils which have shut me out from Thy beauty, and a light that will lead me unto the ocean of Thy Presence.

Let him then raise his hands in supplication toward God—
blessed and exalted be He—and say:†

O Thou the Desire of the world and the Beloved of the nations! Thou seest me turning toward Thee, and rid of all attachment to anyone save Thee, and clinging to Thy cord, through whose movement the whole creation hath been stirred up. I am Thy servant, O my Lord, and the son of Thy servant. Behold me standing ready to do Thy will and Thy desire, and wishing naught else except Thy good pleasure. I implore Thee by the Ocean of Thy mercy and the Day-Star of Thy grace to do with Thy servant as Thou willest and pleasest. By Thy might which is far above all mention and praise! Whatsoever is revealed by Thee is the desire of my heart and the beloved of my soul. O God, my God! Look not upon my hopes and my doings, nay rather look upon Thy will that hath encompassed the heavens and the earth. By Thy Most Great Name, O Thou Lord of all nations! I have desired only what Thou didst desire, and love only what Thou dost love.

---

† "The instruction to raise one's hands occurs once in the medium Obligatory Prayer and five times in the long Obligatory Prayer. The term used in the original Arabic for the first, second and fourth occasions in the long Prayer is the same as that used in the medium Prayer. Therefore it would be entirely correct for the worshipper, when raising his hands on these occasions during the recitation of the long Obligatory Prayer to follow the more specific instructions given in English by the Guardian in his translation of the medium one. On the third and fifth occasions the instruction is given in the long Prayer, the words 'in supplication' are omitted. The House of Justice does not wish at this time to give any specific guidance in this connection; it leaves the matter to the discretion of the friends." (On behalf of the Universal House of Justice, *Lights of Guidance*, p. 468).

Let him then kneel, and bowing his forehead to the ground, let him say:

Exalted art Thou above the description of anyone save Thyself, and the comprehension of aught else except Thee.

Let him then stand and say:

Make my prayer, O my Lord, a fountain of living waters whereby I may live as long as Thy sovereignty endureth, and may make mention of Thee in every world of Thy worlds.

Let him again raise his hands in supplication, and say:

O Thou in separation from Whom hearts and souls have melted, and by the fire of Whose love the whole world hath been set aflame! I implore Thee by Thy Name through which Thou hast subdued the whole creation, not to withhold from me that which is with Thee, O Thou Who rulest over all men! Thou seest, O my Lord, this stranger hastening to his most exalted home beneath the canopy of Thy majesty and within the precincts of Thy mercy; and this transgressor seeking the ocean of Thy forgiveness; and this lowly one the court of Thy glory; and this poor creature the orient of Thy wealth. Thine is the authority to command whatsoever Thou willest. I bear witness that Thou art to be praised in Thy doings, and to be obeyed in Thy behests, and to remain unconstrained in Thy bidding.

Let him then raise his hands, and repeat three times the Greatest Name.[†]
Let him then bend down with hands resting on the knees before God—blessed and exalted be He—and say:

Thou seest, O my God, how my spirit hath been stirred up within my limbs and members, in its longing to worship Thee, and in its yearning to remember Thee and extol Thee; how it testifieth to that whereunto the Tongue of Thy Commandment hath testified in the kingdom of Thine utterance and the heaven of Thy knowledge. I love, in this state, O my Lord, to beg of Thee all that is with Thee, that I may demonstrate my poverty, and magnify Thy bounty and Thy riches, and may declare my powerlessness, and manifest Thy power and Thy might.

---

† "Shoghi Effendi has explained that 'Alláh-u-Abhá' should be used when the Greatest Name is to be repeated three times in the long Obligatory Prayer." (On behalf of the Universal House of Justice, *Lights of Guidance*, p. 467).

Let him then stand and raise his hands twice in supplication, and say:[†]

There is no God but Thee, the Almighty, the All-Bountiful. There is no God but Thee, the Ordainer, both in the beginning and in the end. O God, my God! Thy forgiveness hath emboldened me, and Thy mercy hath strengthened me, and Thy call hath awakened me, and Thy grace hath raised me up and led me unto Thee. Who, otherwise, am I that I should dare to stand at the gate of the city of Thy nearness, or set my face toward the lights that are shining from the heaven of Thy will? Thou seest, O my Lord, this wretched creature knocking at the door of Thy grace, and this evanescent soul seeking the river of everlasting life from the hands of Thy bounty. Thine is the command at all times, O Thou Who art the Lord of all names; and mine is resignation and willing submission to Thy will, O Creator of the heavens!

Let him then raise his hands thrice, and say:[‡]

Greater is God than every great one!

Let him then kneel and, bowing his forehead to the ground, say:

Too high art Thou for the praise of those who are nigh unto Thee to ascend unto the heaven of Thy nearness, or for the birds of the hearts of them who are devoted to Thee to attain to the door of Thy gate. I testify that Thou hast been sanctified above all attributes and holy above all names. No God is there but Thee, the Most Exalted, the All-Glorious.

———————

† "In following the direction stating: 'Let him then stand and raise his hands twice in supplication, and say': . . . the believer does not have to read twice the paragraph which follows. Whether the believer raises his hands twice before the reciting of the paragraph, or commences the reciting after having raised his hands once, and raises them a second time soon thereafter, is left to his choice." (On behalf of the Universal House of Justice, *Lights of Guidance*, p. 467).

‡ "As to the direction which states: 'Let him then raise his hands thrice, and say: . . .', an individual believer asked the beloved Guardian the following question: '. . . the direction to raise the hands thrice and say 'Greater is God than every great one.' Does this mean after every raising of the hands, or only to be said once, after the three raisings?' Shoghi Effendi's secretary answered on his behalf as follows: 'The hands should be raised three times and each time the sentence be repeated in conjunction with the act.'" (On behalf of the Universal House of Justice, *Lights of Guidance*, p. 467).

Let him then seat himself and say:

I testify unto that whereunto have testified all created things, and the Concourse on high, and the inmates of the all-highest Paradise, and beyond them the Tongue of Grandeur itself from the all-glorious Horizon, that Thou art God, that there is no God but Thee, and that He Who hath been manifested is the Hidden Mystery, the Treasured Symbol, through Whom the letters B and E (Be) have been joined and knit together. I testify that it is He Whose name hath been set down by the Pen of the Most High, and Who hath been mentioned in the Books of God, the Lord of the Throne on high and of earth below.

Let him then stand erect and say:

O Lord of all being and Possessor of all things visible and invisible! Thou dost perceive my tears and the sighs I utter, and hearest my groaning, and my wailing, and the lamentation of my heart. By Thy might! My trespasses have kept me back from drawing nigh unto Thee; and my sins have held me far from the court of Thy holiness. Thy love, O my Lord, hath enriched me, and separation from Thee hath destroyed me, and remoteness from Thee hath consumed me. I entreat Thee by Thy footsteps in this wilderness, and by the words "Here am I. Here am I" which Thy chosen Ones have uttered in this immensity, and by the breaths of Thy Revelation, and the gentle winds of the Dawn of Thy Manifestation, to ordain that I may gaze on Thy beauty and observe whatsoever is in Thy Book.

Let him then repeat the Greatest Name thrice,
and bend down with hands resting on the knees, and say:

Praise be to Thee, O my God, that Thou hast aided me to remember Thee and to praise Thee, and hast made known unto me Him Who is the Day-Spring of Thy signs, and hast caused me to bow down before Thy Lordship, and humble myself before Thy Godhead, and to acknowledge that which hath been uttered by the Tongue of Thy grandeur.

Let him then rise and say:

O God, my God! My back is bowed by the burden of my sins, and my heedlessness hath destroyed me. Whenever I ponder my evil doings

82

and Thy benevolence, my heart melteth within me, and my blood boileth in my veins. By Thy Beauty, O Thou the Desire of the world! I blush to lift up my face to Thee, and my longing hands are ashamed to stretch forth toward the heaven of Thy bounty. Thou seest, O my God, how my tears prevent me from remembering Thee and from extolling Thy virtues, O Thou the Lord of the Throne on high and of earth below! I implore Thee by the signs of Thy Kingdom and the mysteries of Thy Dominion to do with Thy loved ones as becometh Thy bounty, O Lord of all being, and is worthy of Thy grace, O King of the seen and the unseen!

Let him then repeat the Greatest Name thrice,
and kneel with his forehead to the ground, and say:

Praise be unto Thee, O our God, that Thou hast sent down unto us that which draweth us nigh unto Thee, and supplieth us with every good thing sent down by Thee in Thy Books and Thy Scriptures. Protect us, we beseech Thee, O my Lord, from the hosts of idle fancies and vain imaginations. Thou, in truth, art the Mighty, the All-Knowing.

Let him then raise his head, and seat himself, and say:

I testify, O my God, to that whereunto Thy chosen Ones have testified, and acknowledge that which the inmates of the all-highest Paradise and those who have circled round Thy mighty Throne have acknowledged. The kingdoms of earth and heaven are Thine, O Lord of the worlds!

(*Prayers and Meditations*, pp. 317-23)

Appendix B

The Authoritative Writings of the Bahá'í Faith

Authoritative Texts of the Bahá'í Faith

The following is a listing of the Bahá'í Faith's major authoritative Writings published in English. The Writings of Bahá'u'lláh, the Báb, and 'Abdu'l-Bahá make up the Sacred Scriptures of the Faith. The writings of 'Abdu'l-Bahá and Shoghi Effendi constitute authoritative interpretations of the Word of God. The letters and messages of the Universal House of Justice provide authoritative guidance and direction for Bahá'ís.

Bahá'u'lláh

1. *The Kitáb-i-Aqdas: The Most Holy Book*
2. *The Kitáb-i-Íqán: The Book of Certitude*
3. *The Hidden Words*
4. *The Seven Valleys and the Four Valleys*
5. *Tablets of Bahá'u'lláh*
6. *Epistle to the Son of the Wolf*
7. *The Proclamation of Bahá'u'lláh*
8. *Gleanings from the Writings of Bahá'u'lláh*
9. *Prayers and Meditations*

The Báb

1. *Selections from the Writings of the Báb*

'Abdu'l-Bahá

1. *Will and Testament of 'Abdu'l-Bahá*
2. *Tablets of the Divine Plan*
3. *Some Answered Questions*
4. *The Secret of Divine Civilization*
5. *Selections from the Writings of 'Abdu'l-Bahá*
6. *A Traveller's Narrative*
7. *Memorials of the Faithful*

In addition to these authoritative texts, the collections of the talks of 'Abdu'l-Bahá are listed and described later in this appendix.

Shoghi Effendi

1. *God Passes By*
2. *The World Order of Bahá'u'lláh* (1929-36)
3. *The Advent of Divine Justice* (1938)
4. *The Promised Day Is Come* (1941)
5. *Bahá'í Administration* (1922-32)
6. *Messages to America* (1932-46)
7. *Citadel of Faith* (1947-57)
8. *Messages to the Bahá'í World* (1950-57)

A listing of the collections of Shoghi Effendi's letters to the Bahá'ís of various countries is provided later in this appendix.

Universal House of Justice

1. *Constitution of the Universal House of Justice*
2. *Wellspring of Guidance* (1963-68)
3. *Messages from the Universal House of Justice* (1968-73)
4. *Messages from the Universal House of Justice: 1963-1986*
5. *A Wider Horizon* (1983-92)
6. *The Promise of World Peace* (1985)
7. *Individual Rights and Freedoms in the World Order of Bahá'u'lláh* (1988)
8. *The Holy Year: 1992-1993*
9. *The Four Year Plan: Messages of the Universal House of Justice* (1996)
10. *Rights & Responsibilities* (1997)

Compilations of Authoritative Writings

In addition to the above texts, a number of topical compilations are available which bring together quotations from the Bahá'í Writings on a single subject. Most of these compilations have been published as separate pamphlets. Nearly all are contained in the two-volume series *Compilation of Compilations*. The topics of the compilations include:

Bahá'í Education	Bahá'í Elections
The Bahá'í Funds	Bahá'í Meetings
Bahíyyih Khánum	Centres of Bahá'í Learning
Chaste and Holy Life	Conservation of the Earth's Resources
Consultation	The Covenant
Crisis and Victory	Deepening
Divorce	Excellence in All Things
Family Life	Health and Healing
Ḥuqúqu'lláh	The Individual and Teaching
Living the Life	The Local Spiritual Assembly
Music	National Convention
The National Spiritual Assembly	Nineteen Day Feast
Peace	The Power of Divine Assistance
Preserving Bahá'í Marriages	Spiritual Foundations
Teaching the Masses	Teaching Prominent People
Trustworthiness	The Universal House of Justice
Women	Youth

Ordering Bahá'í Books

Books may be ordered through local Bahá'í librarians or directly through the Bahá'í Distribution Service:

5397 Wilbanks Dr.
Chattanooga, TN 37343
(800) 999-9019
email: bds@usbnc.org

Descriptions of Authoritative Texts

Writings of Bahá'u'lláh

1. *The Kitáb-i-Aqdas (The Most Holy Book).* ". . . the Kitáb-i-Aqdas is the Charter of the future world civilization that Bahá'u'lláh has come to raise up."[214] It is "the Mother Book of His Revelation, His 'Most Holy Book', the Book in which He sets forth the Laws of God for a Dispensation destined to endure for no less than a thousand years."[215]

Bahá'u'lláh revealed the *Kitáb-i-Aqdas* around the year 1873 while He was imprisoned in 'Akká.[216] In addition to setting forth the laws and ordinances of His World Order, Bahá'u'lláh in the *Kitáb-i-Aqdas* confers upon His Successor, 'Abdu'l-Bahá, the function of interpretation. In this Book, He also ordains the institutions through which the integrity and unity of the Faith can alone be safeguarded.[217]

The Universal House of Justice has described the attitude with which believers should approach the *Kitáb-i-Aqdas*: "May the friends of God ever be mindful of its exalted rank among the sacred texts of the Faith; treasure it as the bread of life; regard possession of it as a sacred honor, as a priceless legacy from the Pen of the Most High, as a source of God's greatest bounty to His creatures; place their whole trust in its provisions; recite its verses; study its contents; adhere to its exhortations; and thus transform their lives in accordance with the divine standard."[218]

2. *The Kitáb-i-Íqán (The Book of Certitude).* The *Kitáb-i-Íqán* "occupies a position unequalled by any work in the entire range of Bahá'í literature, except the Kitáb-i-Aqdas, Bahá'u'lláh's Most Holy Book."[219] It holds a position of "unsurpassed preeminence among the doctrinal"[220] Writings of Bahá'u'lláh. "Well may it be claimed that of all the books revealed by the Author of the Bahá'í Revelation, this Book alone, by sweeping away the age-long barriers that have so insurmountably separated the great religions of the world, has laid down a broad and unassailable foundation for the complete and permanent reconciliation of their followers."[221]

"Books such as the *Íqán, Some Answered Questions* and *The Dawn-Breakers* should be mastered by every Bahá'í. They should read these books over and over again. The first two books will reveal to them the significance of this divine revelation as well as the unity of all the Prophets

88

of old."[222] Further, "The one who ponders over that book [the *Kitáb-i-Íqán*] and grasps its full significance will obtain a clear insight into the old scriptures and appreciate the true mission of the Báb and Bahá'u'lláh."[223]

3. *The Hidden Words*. Bahá'u'lláh has Himself described the *Hidden Words*: "This is that which hath descended from the realm of glory, uttered by the tongue of power and might, and revealed unto the Prophets of old. We have taken the inner essence thereof and clothed it in the garment of brevity, as a token of grace unto the righteous, that they may stand faithful unto the Covenant of God, may fulfill in their lives His trust, and in the realm of spirit obtain the gem of Divine virtue."[224]

The *Hidden Words* is the preeminent *ethical* writing of Bahá'u'lláh, just as the *Kitáb-i-Íqán* is His preeminent *doctrinal* writing, and the *Seven Valleys* is His greatest *mystical* composition.[225] The *Hidden Words* is the "dynamic spiritual leaven cast into the life of the world for the reorientation of the minds of men, the edification of their souls and the rectification of their conduct. . . ."[226]

'Abdu'l-Bahá declares, "Be assured in thyself that if thou dost conduct thyself in accordance with the *Hidden Words* revealed in Persian and in Arabic, thou shalt become a torch of fire of the love of God, an embodiment of humility, of lowliness, of evanescence and of selflessness."[227]

4. *The Seven Valleys and the Four Valleys*. The *Seven Valleys* may well be regarded as Bahá'u'lláh's "greatest mystical composition."[228] In it He "describes the seven stages which the soul of the seeker must needs traverse ere it can attain the object of its existence,"[229] the "stages that mark the wayfarer's journey from the abode of dust to the heavenly homeland."[230] This is the spiritual journey undertaken by all of us.

The *Four Valleys*, also written in a mystical style, is a separate work by Bahá'u'lláh.[231]

5. *Tablets of Bahá'u'lláh*. The tablets contained in *Tablets of Bahá'u'lláh* "must rank among the choicest fruits which His mind has yielded, and mark the consummation of His forty-year-long ministry."[232] These tablets set forth precepts and principles "which lie at the very core of His Faith," reaffirm "truths He had previously proclaimed," elaborate "some of the laws He had already laid down," reveal "further prophecies and warnings," and establish "subsidiary ordinances designed to supplement the provisions of His Most Holy Book."[233] Referring to some of the Writings contained in this book, 'Abdu'l-Bahá has written, "In these Tablets will ye have a model of how to be and how to live."[234]

Tablets of Bahá'u'lláh contains the "Book of the Covenant," which is a document that has "no parallel in the Scriptures of any previous Dispensation."[235] In the "Book of the Covenant," Bahá'u'lláh established His Covenant, commanding all to turn "their faces towards the Most Mighty Branch ['Abdu'l-Bahá],"[236] as the successor of Bahá'u'lláh. *Tablets of Bahá'u'lláh* also includes the "Tablet of Carmel," which is the Charter of the World Center of the Faith. Through this tablet, Bahá'u'lláh has released spiritual forces that have led to the "development of the institutions of the Faith at its World Centre."[237] "The Most Holy Tablet," Bahá'u'lláh's tablet to the Christians, is also among the Writings in the book.

6. ***Epistle to the Son of the Wolf.*** *Epistle to the Son of the Wolf* is the "last outstanding Tablet revealed by the pen of Bahá'u'lláh."[238] The *Epistle*, which was revealed in the last year of Bahá'u'lláh's life, is a lengthy letter addressed to a leading Muslim clergyman, named by Bahá'u'lláh "the Son of the Wolf," who was responsible for the murder of many believers. In the *Epistle*, Bahá'u'lláh calls upon him to "repent of his acts, quotes some of the most characteristic and celebrated passages of His own writings, and adduces proofs establishing the validity of His Cause."[239] Although this work is addressed to a particular individual, in a real sense, it is directed to all of humanity because in it Bahá'u'lláh sets forth the fundamental principles and proofs of His Revelation.

7. ***The Proclamation of Bahá'u'lláh.*** This book is a collection of letters and passages from the Writings of Bahá'u'lláh addressed to the kings, rulers, and religious leaders of the world, inviting them to heed God's call. Some of these Writings address the rulers collectively. Others individually address leaders such as Queen Victoria, Napoleon III, Kaiser Wilhelm, Czar Nicholas, Sulṭán 'Abdu'l-Azíz, the Rulers of America and the Presidents of its Republics, Pope Pius IX, and Chris-

tian, Muslim, and Zoroastrian ecclesiastics. Bahá'u'lláh states, "Never since the beginning of the world hath the Message been so openly proclaimed."[240] 'Abdu'l-Bahá acclaimed these tablets as a "miracle."[241]

In these passages Bahá'u'lláh calls upon the kings and rulers to turn toward the "Most Great Law"; proclaims Himself to be "the King of Kings" and "the Desire of all Nations"; and declares them to be His "vassals" and "emblems of His sovereignty."[242] He also clearly prophesies the downfall of a number of these leaders, including Napoleon III. This summons to the rulers of the world "stands unparalleled in the annals of any previous religion."[243]

8. *Gleanings from the Writings of Bahá'u'lláh.* *Gleanings* consists of "a selection of the most characteristic and hitherto unpublished passages from the outstanding works of the Author of the Bahá'í Revelation."[244] These passages deal with many different subjects, including the Day of God, the Manifestations of God, the soul and its immortality, spiritual aspects of World Order, the Most Great Peace, the duties of the individual, and the spiritual meaning of life. In a statement on his behalf, Shoghi Effendi remarked that *Gleanings* "should be the continued guide and companion of every believer, specially those who are actively engaged in teaching the Cause."[245] Moreover, "The book of 'Gleanings' gives the friends a splendid opportunity to acquire" the "necessary knowledge and understanding" to teach the Message, and gives "that inspiration and spiritual fervor which the reading of the Holy Words can alone impart."[246]

9. *Prayers and Meditations.* *Prayers and Meditations* is a collection of 184 prayers and meditations revealed by Bahá'u'lláh. In a letter written on his behalf, Shoghi Effendi stated that he had "every hope that the perusal of such a precious volume will help to deepen, *more than any other publication*, the spirit of devotion and faith in the friends, and thus charge them with all the spiritual power they require for the accomplishment of their tremendous duties towards the Cause."[247]

Writings of the Báb

1. *Selections from the Writings of the Báb.* This work, which is a collection of the Writings of the Báb, includes excerpts from the

91

Qayyúmu'l-Asmá', "the first, the greatest, and mightiest of all books" of the Dispensation of the Báb;[248] the *Persian Bayán*, "that monumental repository of the laws and precepts of the new Dispensation and the treasury enshrining most of the Báb's references and tributes to . . . 'Him Whom God will make manifest' [Bahá'u'lláh]";[249] the *Seven Proofs*, "original in conception, unanswerable in its arguments, . . . [giving] many and divers proofs of His mission";[250] epistles to Muḥammad Sháh, the King of Persia; and passages from many other Writings and prayers of the Báb.

Writings of 'Abdu'l-Bahá

1. *Will and Testament of 'Abdu'l-Bahá.* The *Will and Testament of 'Abdu'l-Bahá* is "the Charter of a future world civilization, which may be regarded in some of its features as supplementary to no less weighty a Book than the Kitáb-i-Aqdas."[251] It is the "Charter which called into being, outlined the features and set in motion the processes of, this Administrative Order."[252] In it 'Abdu'l-Bahá proclaims the fundamental beliefs of Bahá'ís; reveals the two-fold character of the mission of the Báb; discloses the full station of Bahá'u'lláh; establishes the institution of the Guardianship; defines the scope of the Universal House of Justice, its relationship to the Guardian, and its method of election; and praises the indestructible Covenant of Bahá'u'lláh.[253] The *Will and Testament* is 'Abdu'l-Bahá's "greatest legacy to posterity, the brightest emanation of His mind."[254]

2. *Tablets of the Divine Plan.* *Tablets of the Divine Plan* is the "divine charter of teaching"[255] embodying the Plan that is one of "the two greatest legacies"[256] left by 'Abdu'l-Bahá. It is a collection of fourteen tablets revealed by 'Abdu'l-Bahá in 1916 and 1917, most of which are addressed to the Bahá'ís of the United States and Canada. In these tablets, 'Abdu'l-Bahá "unfolded to their eyes His conception of their spiritual destiny, His Plan for the mission He wished them to undertake,"[257] the mission "to diffuse the light, and erect the administrative fabric, of the Faith throughout the five continents of the globe."[258] The Universal House of Justice has explained that in the arena of teaching, these tablets are the "indispensable terms of reference and the unerring resource"[259] for American Bahá'ís. Shoghi Effendi's letters entitled "The Challeng-

ing Requirements of the Present Hour" and "American Bahá'ís in the Time of World Peril" (both contained in the book *Citadel of Faith*), and *The Advent of Divine Justice*, are invaluable guides that explain the mission 'Abdu'l-Bahá set forth in the *Tablets of the Divine Plan*.[260]

3. *Some Answered Questions*. 'Abdu'l-Bahá's *Some Answered Questions* is "that celebrated compilation of His table talks . . . given during the brief time He was able to spare, in the course of which certain fundamental aspects of His Father's Faith were elucidated, traditional and rational proofs of its validity adduced, and a great variety of subjects regarding the Christian Dispensation, the Prophets of God, Biblical prophecies, the origin and condition of man and other kindred themes authoritatively explained."[261] Laura Clifford Barney recorded 'Abdu'l-Bahá's responses to her questions, which He later reviewed and corrected. Thus, *Some Answered Questions* has the status of an authoritative writing, different from the other non-authoritative talks of 'Abdu'l-Bahá.[262] It is a book that "should be mastered by every Bahá'í."[263]

4. *The Secret of Divine Civilization*. *The Secret of Divine Civilization* is "'Abdu'l-Bahá's outstanding contribution to the future reorganization of the world."[264] It is a message to the government and people of Persia on the essentials of civilization. In it 'Abdu'l-Bahá discusses the role of religion, government, law and justice in a divine society.

5. *Selections from the Writings of 'Abdu'l-Bahá*. *Selections from the Writings of 'Abdu'l-Bahá* presents over 200 selections from 'Abdu'l-Bahá's writings, many of them letters addressed to individual believers, Bahá'í groups, and Assemblies. In these passages, 'Abdu'l-Bahá discusses topics such as the soul and immortality, education, the Manifestations of God, unity, teaching, tests and trials, health and healing, Christian subjects, spiritual qualities, the Covenant, and many others.

6. *A Traveller's Narrative*. This book, written by 'Abdu'l-Bahá, is "the ablest and most valuable presentation of the early history of the Faith and of its tenets."[265] In it He describes the history of the life of the Báb and the early development of the Faith.

7. *Memorials of the Faithful.* This work is a collection of biographical sketches by 'Abdu'l-Bahá of more than seventy of the early believers of the Faith.

Talks of 'Abdu'l-Bahá

There exists a difference in the Faith between the authoritative Writings of Bahá'u'lláh, the Báb, and 'Abdu'l-Bahá, and their oral statements. Only the former are considered authoritative and binding. "Bahá'u'lláh has made it clear enough that only those things that have been revealed in the form of Tablets have a binding power over the friends. . . . This being a basic principle of the Faith we should not confuse Tablets that were actually revealed and mere talks attributed to the founders of the Cause."[266] Thus, although the following collections of 'Abdu'l-Bahá's talks are of profound interest to the student of the Faith, they do not have the status of authoritative Writings.

1. *The Promulgation of Universal Peace.* *The Promulgation* is a collection of 'Abdu'l-Bahá's talks during His eight-month long teaching tour throughout the United States and Canada in 1912. His talks were given before Bahá'í and non-Bahá'í audiences, such as at the Fourth Annual Conference of the N.A.A.C.P., at Stanford University, in numerous churches and synagogues, and before various social groups. Shoghi Effendi has commented upon 'Abdu'l-Bahá's presentations in America and Europe: "It was in the course of these epoch-making journeys and before large and representative audiences, at times exceeding a thousand people, that 'Abdu'l-Bahá expounded, with brilliant simplicity, with persuasiveness and force, and for the first time in His ministry, those basic and distinguishing principles of His Father's Faith. . . ."[267]

2. *Paris Talks.* *Paris Talks* is a collection of talks delivered by 'Abdu'l-Bahá during His stay in Paris in 1911. These talks discuss many social and spiritual principles of Bahá'u'lláh.

3. *'Abdu'l-Bahá in London.* This book is a collection of addresses and notes of conversations of 'Abdu'l-Bahá during His stay in London in 1911.

Writings of Shoghi Effendi, the Guardian of the Faith

1. *God Passes By*. *God Passes By* is Shoghi Effendi's survey of the outstanding events of the Faith's first century, from 1844-1944. It is arguably the most important historical account of the first one hundred years of the Bahá'í Faith. In it he reviews the ministries of the Báb (1844-1853), of Bahá'u'lláh (1853-1892), and of 'Abdu'l-Bahá (1892-1921), and the inception of the Formative Age of the Bahá'í Faith (1921-1944). The Guardian not only discusses the outstanding events in the birth of the Faith and of its Administrative Order, he also examines and outlines all the major Writings of the three Central Figures of the Faith. Thus, the book may be used as an essential tool for study of the Bahá'í Writings. *God Passes By* is the only book that Shoghi Effendi wrote in his life; the rest of his writings are in the form of letters.

2. *The World Order of Bahá'u'lláh*. A collection of seven lengthy letters written by the Guardian from 1929 through 1936, and addressed to the Bahá'ís of the West, make up the book *The World Order of Bahá'u'lláh*. An understanding of these letters is fundamental to an understanding of the changes taking place in the world through the establishment of Bahá'u'lláh's World Order. Among the most important of these letters is one entitled "The Dispensation of Bahá'u'lláh." In this letter, the Guardian explains "certain truths which lie at the basis of our Faith and the integrity of which it is our first duty to safeguard."[268] These truths include the significance of the stations and relationships of Bahá'u'lláh, the Báb, and 'Abdu'l-Bahá, and the purpose and function of the Administrative Order. The "Dispensation of Bahá'u'lláh" is "an invaluable supplement"[269] to Bahá'u'lláh's "Book of the Covenant" and the *Will and Testament of 'Abdu'l-Bahá*. Shoghi Effendi is reported to have remarked that "he had said all he had to say, in many ways, in the *Dispensation*."[270]

The other letters contained in *The World Order of Bahá'u'lláh* explore the distinguishing features of the Faith, aspects of the Administrative Order and the World Order, the destiny of America, and the unfoldment of divine civilization.

3. *The Advent of Divine Justice*. *The Advent of Divine Justice* is a letter by Shoghi Effendi written in 1938, addressed to the Bahá'ís of the

United States and Canada. It describes the role and destiny of the American Bahá'í community, how that destiny can be fulfilled, and what obstacles American Bahá'ís must overcome. It explains the Bahá'í response and solution to the problems of racial prejudice, political corruption, and moral laxity. *The Advent* is also a "how to" guide for teaching: the spiritual prerequisites for success in teaching, the teaching requirements at home and abroad, and the practical methods of teaching.

4. *The Promised Day Is Come.* *The Promised Day is Come* is a letter written by the Guardian in 1941 during the Second World War. In it he discusses the ordeal that has gripped mankind as a judgment of God against the peoples of the earth who for a century have refused to recognize Bahá'u'lláh, He Who is the Promise of All Ages. He enumerates the woeful trials that afflicted the Central Figures of the Faith; the responsibility of the sovereigns and religious leaders of the world; the warnings addressed to them by Bahá'u'lláh; and the punishments many of these leaders have suffered. *The Promised Day is Come* also explains how God's divine justice not only punishes, but is "a disciplinary and creative process, whose aim is the salvation, through unification, of the entire planet."[271]

5. *Bahá'í Administration.* *Bahá'í Administration* is a collection of Shoghi Effendi's letters, addressed during 1922-1932 to Bahá'ís of the United States and Canada. The Guardian nurtures our understanding and appreciation of Bahá'í Administration and our duty in serving it. These letters explain the origin, nature, and functioning of the Administrative Order of the Faith and discuss such topics as the Universal House of Justice, National and Local Spiritual Assemblies, conventions, the Bahá'í Fund, the Mashriqu'l-Adhkár (House of Worship), elections, consultation, and teaching.

6. *Messages to America.* *Messages to America* is a collection of letters written by the Guardian between 1932 and 1946, addressed to the Bahá'ís of the United States and Canada through their national institutions. Many of these letters were written during the Second World War when the American Bahá'í community was engaged in the first Seven Year Teaching Plan.

7. *Citadel of Faith*. This book is a collection of letters written between 1947 and 1957 and addressed to the American Bahá'í community. In these letters, the Guardian describes the world mission of that community and reminds it of its spiritual primacy in carrying out 'Abdu'l-Bahá's Divine Plan. Two of the most important letters contained in *Citadel of Faith* are "The Challenging Requirements of the Present Hour" and "American Bahá'ís in the Time of World Peril," which are invaluable guides in explaining the mission 'Abdu'l-Bahá set forth in the *Tablets of the Divine Plan*.[272]

8. *Messages to the Bahá'í World*. *Messages to the Bahá'í World* is a collection of letters written between 1950 and 1957 addressed to the worldwide Bahá'í community. These letters call upon Bahá'ís to participate, for the first time, in a world-encompassing teaching plan, the Ten Year Spiritual Crusade. They also discuss such topics as the Covenant and Covenant-breaking, the development of the International Bahá'í Council, the institution of the Hands of the Cause, and other subjects. *Messages to the Bahá'í World* also contains Shoghi Effendi's last general letter to the Bahá'ís of the world, written only a few weeks before his passing in November 1957.

9. Other collections of letters written by Shoghi Effendi
a. *Arohanui*—messages to the Bahá'ís of New Zealand
b. *Messages of Shoghi Effendi to the Indian Subcontinent*—messages to the Bahá'ís of India
c. *High Endeavors*—messages to the Bahá'ís of Alaska
d. *Messages to the Antipodes*—messages to the Bahá'ís of Australasia
e. *Japan Will Turn Ablaze!*—messages to the Bahá'ís of Japan (also contains Tablets and talks by 'Abdu'l-Bahá)
f. *Light of Divine Guidance* (vol. I & II)—messages to the Bahá'ís of Germany and Austria
g. *Messages to Canada*—messages to the Bahá'ís of Canada
h. *Unfolding Destiny*—messages to the Bahá'ís of the British Isles

10. *The Dawn-Breakers: Nabíl's Narrative*. *The Dawn-Breakers* is not part of the authoritative Writings of the Faith, as it was a narrative written by Nabíl, one of the early believers living in the days of the Báb and Bahá'u'lláh; however, it occupies a unique position in Bahá'í literature. Parts of the narrative were read to Bahá'u'lláh and revised by 'Abdu'l-Bahá, and the work was edited and translated by Shoghi Effendi. It is one of the books that "should be mastered by every Bahá'í."[273] Shoghi Effendi has written, "Indeed the chief motive actuating me to undertake the task of editing and translating Nabíl's immortal Narrative has been to enable every follower of the Faith in the West to better understand and more readily grasp the tremendous implications of His [the Báb's] exalted station and to more ardently admire and love Him."[274]

Writings of the Universal House of Justice

1. *Constitution of the Universal House of Justice*. The *Constitution*, signed in 1972, sets forth the purpose and function of the Universal House of Justice and enumerates its powers and duties. This document also includes bylaws bearing upon such matters as membership in the Bahá'í community; the Local and National Spiritual Assemblies and the obligations of their members; Bahá'í elections; the right of review; appeals; the Board of Counsellors; and the Auxiliary Boards.

The Constitution was envisaged in the writings of the Guardian, who hailed it as "the Most Great Law of the Faith of Bahá'u'lláh."[275]

2. *Wellspring of Guidance*. *Wellspring of Guidance* is a collection of messages of the Universal House of Justice written between 1963 and 1968 to Bahá'ís and Bahá'í institutions around the world. It contains the first statement of the Universal House of Justice after its formation in April 1963. The compilation contains important letters on such topics as the Guardianship and the Universal House of Justice, teaching, the Hands of the Cause, observance of Bahá'í holy days, youth, the relationship of Bahá'ís to politics, and other subjects.

3. *Messages from the Universal House of Justice (1968-73)*. This book is a compilation of communications of the Universal House of Justice written between 1968 and 1973, addressed to Bahá'ís and Bahá'í institutions. Among the subjects of these messages are the Guardianship and the Universal House of Justice, the Continental Board of Counselors and the Auxiliary Board, teaching, pioneering and education, laws regarding sexual conduct, noninterference in political activities, consultation, elimination of prejudice, the Bahá'í Fund, self-defense, and other matters.

4. *Messages from the Universal House of Justice: 1963-1986.* This recently published work provides the most comprehensive compilation of the messages of the Universal House of Justice ever published in English. The book's more than 450 messages, spanning from 1963 through 1986, cover the Nine Year, the Five Year, and the Seven Year Plans. Addressed to Bahá'í institutions, groups, and individuals, these statements by the House of Justice provide a wealth of divine guidance on the spiritual, social, and administrative principles guiding the development of the Faith. In addition to including many previously unpublished messages, this compilation contains all of the messages published in *Wellspring of Guidance* and all but six messages published in *Messages from the Universal House of Justice (1968-1973)*.

5. *A Wider Horizon.* *A Wider Horizon* is a collection of letters of the Universal House of Justice written during the period 1983 through 1992. It includes the annual Riḍván letters of the House of Justice addressed to the Bahá'ís of the world. It also includes guidance on such topics as social and economic development, the Bahá'í Fund, youth, the Fourth Epoch of the Formative Age, the Arc Projects, Nineteen Day Feast, and other issues.

6. *The Promise of World Peace.* *The Promise of World Peace* is a statement by the Universal House of Justice written in 1985 during the International Year of Peace and addressed "To the Peoples of the World." It presents the Bahá'í perspective on the attainment of world peace. This statement has been presented to heads of governments, leaders of thought, jurists, academics, religious figures, and various organizations. The Universal House of Justice, in referring to *The Promise of World Peace*, has written, "Its delivery to national governmental leaders having been virtually completed, its contents must now be conveyed, by all possible means, to peoples everywhere from all walks of life. This is a necessary part of the teaching work in our time and must be pursued with unabated vigor."[276]

7. *Individual Rights and Freedoms in the World Order of Bahá'u'lláh*. *Individual Rights and Freedoms* is a letter written in 1988, addressed to the followers of Bahá'u'lláh in the United States. It explains the Bahá'í concept of freedom, how it differs from western notions of liberty, and what its characteristics and expressions should be within the Bahá'í community.

8. *The Holy Year: 1992-1993*. This is a compilation of the messages of the Universal House of Justice during the Holy Year, 1992-1993. The compilation includes the messages presented at that year's significant events, including the commemoration in the Holy Land of the hundredth anniversary of the ascension of Bahá'u'lláh, as well as the Second Bahá'í World Congress in New York.

9. *The Four Year Plan: Messages of the Universal House of Justice*. This book contains the major messages of the Universal House of Justice relating to the Four Year Plan, which spans from 1996 to the year 2000. Among these messages are the Ridván letter to the Bahá'ís of the World and eight letters addressed to "the believers in each continent of the globe, or parts thereof, exploring the implications of the Four Year Plan in the light of the particular conditions of their countries."[277]

10. *Rights & Responsibilities*. This booklet contains messages of the Universal House of Justice on the subject of the relationship between individuals and Bahá'í institutions. The messages address the Bahá'í view of freedom of speech and the role of criticism, among other topics.

Practical Ideas for
Studying the Bahá'í Writings

General Approach to Study

As discussed earlier, studying the Faith is the sacred obligation of every believer. In fulfilling this obligation, one has to be aware of the spiritual insights related to study. Moreover, it is necessary to learn the skills of effective study. The purpose of this appendix is to discuss how one may acquire such skills. Developing study skills is a goal that can easily be reached through a little practice and discipline. Anyone who can read this page already has the capacity to study.

One of the first steps in learning how to study is arousing the desire to study. We can arouse this desire through our love for the Faith, through praying, meditating, or being inspired by the positive impact that study has had on the lives of other believers. The act of study itself encourages a greater desire to study. Once we have committed ourselves to studying the Faith, it is best to proceed systematically. Study is not very effective if it is done in a random or disorderly manner. The approach of "I'll read a few pages of whatever book catches my eye that day" is unlikely to lead to an adequate understanding of the Faith.

The word "systematic" suggests that one should have a plan and strive to be regular, methodical, and thorough. Our study must have an order and a direction to it, in terms of what and how we study. For example, we can be systematic by regularly reading a book or a series of books. One can be systematic by reading each day a set number of pages or reading for a set period of time. As mentioned above, by simply reading 16 pages per day, one can systematically cover in one year the Faith's major Writings presently available in English (or do so in two years by reading approximately eight pages per day).

However, our object is not simply to quickly run through all the Writings, but to explore their depth as well. If we hurriedly read all the Writings without reflecting on them, we may have lots of knowledge but little understanding. On the other hand, if we study deeply only a narrow selection of passages, we may have a good understanding of a few principles, but fail to see how they relate to the whole. A balance between the two is required. One approach is to fairly quickly read a book and then go back and reflect more deeply on certain portions. Another approach is to set aside a period of time each day for study. Some days a great many pages may be read, while other days, only a few, because of the density of the material or because the student spends time reflecting back on what has been read previously.

In addition to taking a systematic approach, it is also a good idea to begin modestly, to start out with a small, manageable goal. Sometimes Bahá'ís get very excited about study and set ambitious and unrealistic goals for themselves: "I will study four hours every day!" One may well have the capacity to study four hours per day; however, if he has never done this before, it is not very likely he will succeed at suddenly going from zero hours of study to four hours of study per day.

Rather, it may be wiser to set a goal that one can reasonably achieve. For example, a believer may decide to commit to studying 15 minutes per day. Because this is a manageable goal, it can be fulfilled regardless of the other obligations one may have. Even if one is busy, has to work, has an exam, or is going to the movies that day, one can still manage to find 15 minutes to study. Once this study period has become a regular part of one's life, it then can be increased to 20 minutes and then to 30 minutes, and gradually to an hour and more. Most students of the Writings find that they need more and more time for study because of the absorbing nature of the materials.

Studying in the same place and at the same time each day will also help to establish the pattern of regular study. We may ask ourselves, "What time of the day can I devote to study, so that this period becomes 'sacred,' that is, a time that will not be interrupted by telephone calls, family and friends, television, etc.?"

Specific Techniques of Study

As the practice of study becomes an established part of our lives, we will want to improve its quality, so that we can get the most out of the time we spend. Probably, reading is the simplest technique of study. Reading straight through a book, without taking notes or checking other sources, is an excellent first step. This allows one to get "the big picture." One misses many details in the process, but that is okay because these can be discovered through subsequent readings.

The Writings of Bahá'u'lláh, the Báb, 'Abdu'l-Bahá, Shoghi Effendi, and the Universal House of Justice have very different styles. One has to become accustomed to the style and flavor of each. At first reading, the Writings of Bahá'u'lláh or Shoghi Effendi may be difficult. It may be wise to begin with those Writings that one finds easier to understand (e.g. setting a goal to read all of 'Abdu'l-Bahá's Writings). However, we must eventually tackle the more challenging works and find our way through all the Writings. Studying a few pages at a time, writing the definitions of unfamiliar words in the margins, and asking questions from, or studying with, more experienced believers are ways in which we can approach the books that may initially seem difficult.

It should be noted that the student should make a clear distinction in his mind between the Faith's primary literature (those by Bahá'u'lláh, the Báb, 'Abdu'l-Bahá, Shoghi Effendi, and the Universal House of Justice) and secondary literature, written by others about the Faith. Although the secondary literature may help us to understand the Faith, the major focus of our study must remain the primary literature. Otherwise, we are not investigating and seeing the Faith through our own eyes, but are getting it secondhand through the eyes of others. However, when the student has a solid grounding in the primary literature, then he can better weigh the opinions of other authors against the standards of the Teachings.

There are many methods we can use to improve our reading. How often have we read a whole page, and when we have reached the end of the page, we cannot remember a single thing we have read? Our eyes have moved over the words, but the concepts have not entered into our minds. One of the ways that we can improve our concentration while reading is by underlining or circling key words in the text as we are going through a paragraph. Another technique is summarizing in two

103

or three words the theme of the paragraph we have just read. We can write the summaries in the margins of the book or on separate sheets of paper. Below is a listing of some study techniques. Obviously, not everyone will use all of these techniques. Try them, and determine which ones are of benefit to you. (Note: Some of the techniques listed below are illustrated in the sample page that follows this discussion. These are marked with an asterisk*.)

*1. taking notes in the margins of the book or in a separate notebook
*2. highlighting, underlining, or circling key words and phrases
*3. numbering the different points that appear in a paragraph; listing these items (e.g. Four purposes of the Covenant are . . . [See God Passes By, pp. 244-45])
4. examining the title, subtitles, preface, and index of a book
5. reviewing what one has read ("What can I recall from what I read yesterday?")
*6. summarizing each paragraph of the text in a few words (e.g. "Functions of Guardian and House of Justice")
7. making an outline of the text
*8. cross-referencing sources (e.g. "cf. ADJ, p. 15." or "This topic also discussed in Advent of Divine Justice, p. 15")
9. compiling one's favorite quotations in a notebook
10. compiling quotations on different subjects (e.g. justice, prayer, life after death, unity, etc.)
11. learning the meanings of words by using a secular dictionary or discovering their definitions by seeing how they are used in other passages of the Bahá'í Writings
*12. writing definitions of words in the margins
13. memorizing key passages
14. pondering on the implications and applications of a passage (e.g. "How practically can I apply this to my life?" "How does this principle relate to what I read in that other book?" "Why did Bahá'u'lláh reveal this law?")
15. using study guides
16. using 3 x 5 flash cards for learning/memorization
17. formulating study questions based on the text (e.g. One who layeth claim to a Revelation direct from God, ere the expiration of how

many years is assuredly a lying imposter? [*See Kitáb-i-Aqdas*, parag. 37])

18. keeping a list of questions one has about the Faith or about a book (These questions can be answered through further reading and research. One can also seek answers to these questions when one meets a well-read believer.)

19. creating one's own study guides

20. creating files for different subjects (e.g. creating files on teaching, race unity, etc. Whenever one comes across new materials relating to that subject, they are put into that file.)

21. maintaining a file or notebook of the Universal House of Justice's messages as they are released

22. finding the sources of quotations (e.g. The quotation "Knowledge is twenty and seven letters. . . ." cited in *The World Order of Bahá'u'lláh*, p. 125, comes from the *Kitáb-i-Íqán*, pp. 243-44)

23. using *God Passes By* as a study guide: In *God Passes By*, Shoghi Effendi summarizes the major Writings of Bahá'u'lláh, the Báb, and 'Abdu'l-Bahá. These summaries, which appear throughout the book, can be used as an authoritative outline of the contents of these Writings. For example, the *Will and Testament of 'Abdu'l-Bahá* is summarized into twenty different points: "The Document . . . [1] proclaims, categorically and unequivocally, the fundamental beliefs of the followers of the Faith of Bahá'u'lláh; [2] reveals, in unmistakable language, the twofold character of the Mission of the Báb; . . . [20] and voices His prayers for the repentance as well as the forgiveness of His enemies." (*God Passes By*, p. 328) An excellent study project is to try to find each of these twenty points in the text of the *Will and Testament* itself.

This is only a sampling of different study techniques. You will develop your own ways and methods. As with the other spiritual practices, the key is to make a small beginning and a daily effort, and progress will soon follow.

THE WORLD ORDER OF BAHA'U'LLAH

in His Will the very term which He Himself had chosen when refuting the argument of the Covenant-breakers who had challenged His right to interpret the utterances of Bahá'u'lláh. "*After him,*" He adds, "*will succeed the first-born of his lineal descendants.*" "*The mighty stronghold,*" He further explains, "*shall remain impregnable and safe through obedience to him who is the Guardian of the Cause of God.*" "*It is incumbent upon the members of the House of Justice, upon all the Aghsán, the Afnán, the Hands of the Cause of God, to show their obedience, submissiveness and subordination unto the Guardian of the Cause of God.*"

"*It is incumbent upon the members of the House of Justice,*" Bahá'u'lláh, on the other hand, declares in the Eighth Leaf of the Exalted Paradise, "*to take counsel together regarding those things which have not outwardly been revealed in the Book, and to enforce that which is agreeable to them. God will verily inspire them with whatsoever He willeth, and He verily is the Provider, the Omniscient.*" "*Unto the Most Holy Book*" (the Kitáb-i-Aqdas), 'Abdu'l-Bahá states in His Will, "*every one must turn, and all that is not expressly recorded therein must be referred to the Universal House of Justice. That which this body, whether unanimously or by a majority doth carry, that is verily the truth and the purpose of God Himself. Whoso doth deviate therefrom is verily of them that love discord, hath shown forth malice, and turned away from the Lord of the Covenant.*"

Not only does 'Abdu'l-Bahá confirm in His Will Bahá'u'lláh's above-quoted statement, but invests this body with the additional right and power to abrogate, according to the exigencies of time, its own enactments, as well as those of a preceding House of Justice. "*Inasmuch as the House of Justice,*" is His explicit statement in His Will, "*hath power to enact laws that are not expressly recorded in the Book and bear upon daily transactions, so also it hath power to repeal the same... This it can do because these laws form no part of the divine explicit text.*"

Referring to both the Guardian and the Universal House of Justice we read these emphatic words: "*The sacred and youthful Branch, the Guardian of the Cause of God, as well as the Universal House of Justice to be universally elected and established, are both under the care and protection of the Abhá Beauty, under the shelter and unerring guidance of the Exalted One (the Báb) (may my life be offered up for them both). Whatsoever they decide is of God.*"

From these statements it is made indubitably clear and evident

[Handwritten margin annotations:]

'Abdu'l-Bahá's Will

male descendants of Bahá'u'lláh

relatives of the Báb

W+T p. ?

defn: abolish, nullify

W+T p. 20

W+T p. 11

Guardianship: succession

?? What is "Eighth Leaf"?

House of Justice: legislation

House of Justice: right to repeal own laws

Guardian + House: protected + guided

106

Appendix D

Teaching Groups:
A Practical Way to Teach

While Bahá'ís are generally aware of the importance of teaching, many of us lack the confidence to teach and feel we do not know what course of action to follow. One easy way believers can teach is by starting or joining a teaching group. By working with others, individuals can overcome their fears and feelings of inadequacy and can learn practically how to teach.

The idea of the teaching group is very simple. A teaching group is formed when a few believers come together and commit themselves to teaching a segment of the public. Through prayer and study of the Writings, the members of the group spiritually prepare themselves to teach. They consult and make a teaching plan. Then they act. After action, they reflect and learn from their experiences and adjust their plans, if necessary, to improve their efforts. The members of the group, either together or each person alone, work to achieve their goals. Thus, the teaching group is continually praying, studying, consulting, acting, and reflecting.

Who can form a teaching group? Any two or more believers can form a group. For example, a group may consist of a mother and son or a whole family or perhaps two families working together. It may be formed by a few friends or a handful of youth. Any type of group is possible.

What will the group do? Some specific activities of teaching groups are discussed below:

1. Prayer and Study: Teaching is more than giving information to others about the Faith. It involves the sacred act of touching another person's heart with the Message of God's Revelation. Because teaching is a spiritual act, it requires spiritual preparation. This preparation comes through praying for divine assistance and through studying the Teachings.

Teaching groups may choose to study those Writings that relate to teaching. Writings such as 'Abdu'l-Bahá's *Tablets of the Divine Plan*, Shoghi Effendi's *Advent of Divine Justice*, the compilations *The Individual and Teaching* (*The Gift of Teaching*), *The Power of Divine Assistance*, and *Entry by Troops* provide spiritual insights into teaching. Books like the *Kitáb-i-Íqán*, *Some Answered Questions*, and *The Promulgation of Universal Peace* arm us with knowledge of principles, proofs, and arguments.

Memorizing the Writings is one of the activities of effective teachers. Reciting memorized passages can help one both in preparing to teach and in the act of teaching itself. Bahá'u'lláh has written, "From the texts of the wondrous, heavenly Scriptures they should memorize phrases and passages bearing on various instances, so that in the course of their speech they may recite divine verses whenever the occasion demandeth it, inasmuch as these holy verses are the most potent elixir, the greatest and mightiest talisman."[278]

2. Consultation: The members of the teaching group should consult on what they will do. This includes deciding whom to teach and how to teach them. Rather than just hoping to teach "everyone," it is helpful for the group to select a particular segment of the public on whom they will focus. This may be an area of a city, an age or ethnic group, a place where people gather, a school or university, people at work, or a special association. Selecting the focus population may depend upon the interests and talents of the members of the teaching group or on the segments of the population to which the members of the group have access.

For example, one group after consultation decided that because the members enjoyed poetry, they would form a poetry appreciation group. They invited non-Bahá'í friends who had the same interest to join them. Some of the poetry that was shared were the Words of Bahá'u'lláh and the Báb. Over time, some of the friends of the Bahá'ís recognized Bahá'u'lláh and joined the Faith. A different teaching group decided that its focus population would be African American youth. They concentrated on teaching this population, and in a short period of time, a number of people become attracted to the Faith and enrolled as believers.

After a focus population has been selected, the members of the teaching group must consult on how to attractively present the Faith to this population. Shoghi Effendi has written that "the fundamental prerequisite for any successful teaching enterprise" is to adapt the presentation of the principles of the Faith to "the cultural and religious backgrounds, the ideologies, and the temperament"[279] of the people we are teaching. To do this, one has to get to know the interests, concerns, customs, and habits of the population and figure out how to present the Faith in an appealing way. Moreover, the group should consider how to apply the Bahá'í Teachings to the issues and problems facing the population (i.e. How does the Faith help the population to resolve its daily issues?)

3. Action and Reflection: The teaching group should not "get stuck" in planning. Rather than spending weeks and weeks on developing a plan and an approach, it is wiser to make a simple plan and immediately take action. Likewise, instead of starting a huge project at first, it may be better to begin in a small way and build up gradually. By carrying out some simple teaching actions, the group can learn whether its plans are headed in the right direction. More importantly, these actions themselves attract the blessings of God.

The teaching efforts of the group should not be isolated events, but each act should build on another. For example, if a group is trying to reach schoolteachers, it may decide to make direct contact with the schoolteachers to share with them the Bahá'í teachings on education. The group may next decide to invite those who have been receptive to a program on education put on by the teaching group. As contacts and friendships are developed, some of the schoolteachers may be invited to dinner to personally discuss the Faith. These actions continue, one building on another.

If, after acting and reflecting, the group finds that a particular strategy is not working, then it can change its plans and try something different. Thus, action leads to reflection, and reflection leads to action. In taking action, the group should use creative approaches and persevere in its efforts, even if the results are not at first promising. In the past, some teaching groups have not continued their efforts because they did not immediately see results. We must recognize that it takes time to learn the skills of teaching. As such, it may be helpful for group members to commit themselves to the endeavor for a certain length of time (e.g. at least one year), so that adequate opportunity is allowed for skills to be developed. Moreover, part of the function that teaching group members can serve is to encourage one another in the face of challenges and failures.

In teaching, a group may realize appropriate literature or materials do not exist for its focus population. The teaching group, as part of its action, may try to develop such materials (e.g. a brief pamphlet).

4. Growth and Consolidation: As those taught become Bahá'ís (or even before they have become Bahá'ís), they can join the teaching group. By being a part of the group, they will learn how to pray, study, consult, and teach, and will become active and contributing members of the Bahá'í community. However, the group should assume responsibility for the deepening of the new believers, whether or not they join the group.

5. Relationship to Institutions: The teaching group is not an administrative institution, but is simply a group of friends who come together to spiritualize themselves and teach the Faith. The group, thus, provides a way for individuals to carry out their personal obligation to teach. As such, up to a point, the teaching group does not need the approval of a Local Spiritual Assembly in order to carry out its activities. However, because the spirit of the Faith is one of collaboration, it is most appropriate for the group to consult with the Assembly and to keep it informed of its activities. If the activities of the teaching group will affect the interests of the public as a whole, Assembly approval is required. If there exists any question, the group should check with the Assembly. Additionally, Auxiliary Board members and their assistants are another valuable resource for the teaching group.

A Step-by-Step Approach to Forming a Teaching Group

Getting Started

1. Members: Who will be the members of our teaching group?
2. Prayer and Study: In addition to having fervent prayers, what will the group study?
3. Consultation:
   a. What segment of the population will the group focus on teaching? (e.g. students at a certain high school; an area of the city; a particular ethnic group; a special interest group; etc.)
   b. What is our strategy for teaching this population? (e.g. through the arts; making contacts with those already known by the members of the teaching group; etc.)
4. Action:
   a. What is the first thing the group will do, either individually or together? (e.g. Each member of the group will visit at least two friends and will invite them to a presentation on the Faith at the home of one of the group members.)
   b. When will this be done?
   c. What can be done after this, so that the actions are not isolated events, but build on one another?
   d. When is the teaching group's next meeting?

Making Progress

Once the teaching group has started, it will come together again for prayers, study, and consultation. The group will need to consider:
1. Memorization: What passages from the Writings can we memorize so that we can become more effective teachers?
2. Reflection/Consultation:
   a. How well did the planned action go? If the action was positive, what can be done to make it even better? If the action did not go well, what different strategies do we want to try?
   b. In order to effectively teach, are there certain skills we need to learn? (e.g. persuasively presenting the Teachings). How can we gain these skills? (e.g. practicing with one another on presenting principles, proofs, arguments, etc.)
3. Action: What is our next action?

Appendix E

Calculation of Ḥuqúqu'lláh

Computation of Ḥuqúqu'lláh

The computation and payment of the Right of God, within the general guidelines that have been given, are "exclusively a matter of conscience between the individual and God."[280] Therefore, if a Bahá'í tries his best, based on his understanding of the Writings, to calculate his Ḥuqúqu'lláh, then he has fulfilled his duty.

Briefly, the law states that nineteen percent of one's capital is payable as Ḥuqúqu'lláh when such capital has reached an amount of at least nineteen mithqáls in gold. (A "mithqál" [roughly pronounced "mess-gall"] is a unit of weight, equivalent to a little over 3.4 grams. Nineteen mithqáls equal 69.192 grams or 2.225 troy ounces.) In determining the amount of Ḥuqúqu'lláh a believer should pay, he must first deduct any debts or expenses he may have and then pay nineteen per cent on the remainder of his capital, if it is equal to at least nineteen mithqáls of gold.

For example, if at the present time, the value of gold is $400 per ounce,[281] then 19 mithqáls, or 2.225 ounces, of gold are worth $890 ($400 x 2.225). One's capital therefore has to equal or exceed $890 in order for Ḥuqúqu'lláh to be payable. Thus, if a Bahá'í has $3,000 and deducts $2,500 in expenses, leaving $500 in capital, then no Ḥuqúqu'lláh would be payable on this $500 because it does not equal or exceed $890. If, on the other hand, one has $3000 and deducts $2110 in expenses, then $890 would remain. The amount of $890 is at least equal to nineteen mithqáls of gold (calculated above to be $890); therefore, 19% of this amount, or $169.10 ($890 x 19%), would be the amount payable as Ḥuqúqu'lláh.

The following are more specific guidelines provided in the Writings on how Huqúqu'lláh should be calculated:[282]

1. Everything that a believer possesses, with the exception of certain items that are exempt, is subject once and only once to the payment of Ḥuqúqu'lláh.

2. The following items are exempt from assessment of Ḥuqúqu'lláh:

    a. The residence and its needful furnishings. (It is left to the discretion of the individual to decide what is "needful" for himself and his family.)
    b. The needful business and agricultural equipment which produce income for one's subsistence.

3. The following items are deductible expenses:

    a. General expenses of living.
    b. Losses and expenses incurred on the sale of possessions.
    c. Sums which are paid to the State, such as taxes and duties.

4. Payment is due on whole units of 19 mi<u>th</u>qáls of gold. (For example, if 19 mi<u>th</u>qáls of gold has a value of $890, and one has assessable capital of $1000, then Ḥuqúqu'lláh is payable only on $890 of that $1,000. The remaining $110 will have to increase to another whole unit of 19 mi<u>th</u>qáls of gold before it would be subject to payment of Ḥuqúqu'lláh.)

5. When a person receives a gift or bequest, it is to be added to his possessions and augments the total value in the same way as does an excess of annual income over expenditures.

6. If property increases in value, Ḥuqúqu'lláh is not payable on that increase until it is realized (e.g. through the sale of the property).

7. If possessions decrease, such as through the expenses of a year exceeding the income received, Ḥuqúqu'lláh falls due again only after the loss has been made good and the total value of one's assessable possessions is augmented.

8. The time and method of payment of Ḥuqúqu'lláh are left to the discretion of the individual. There is, therefore, no obligation to

liquidate one's assets in haste in order to fulfill one's current obligations to Ḥuqúqu'lláh.

9. Husband and wife are free to decide whether they want to honor their Ḥuqúqu'lláh obligations jointly or individually.

10. Payment of the Ḥuqúqu'lláh has priority over making contributions to the Funds of the Faith. It is left to the discretion of the believer whether to treat contributions to the Fund as an expense in calculating deductions.

11. Ḥuqúqu'lláh is paid to the Trustee of Ḥuqúqu'lláh, his Deputies, or their appointed Representatives. These persons issue receipts and forward the funds to the Universal House of Justice.

Sample Calculation

Individual believers will calculate Ḥuqúqu'lláh in different ways, depending upon their understanding of the Bahá'í Writings and the complexity of their personal affairs. Beyond the general principles discussed above, no particular method of calculation has been prescribed in the Writings. A Ḥuqúqu'lláh calculation is presented below as an example only of one possible method by which a Bahá'í may determine her Ḥuqúqu'lláh.

Jackie desires to determine the amount of her Ḥuqúqu'lláh. The following explains her financial situation:

ASSETS SHE OWNS:
1. A residence worth $50,000.
2. Needful household furnishings worth $5,000.
3. A $5,000 car, which she uses in her business.
4. Stocks worth $2,000.
5. A savings account worth $700.

HER EARNINGS AND EXPENSES THIS YEAR:
6. Her salary was $25,000 this year.
7. She paid $6000 in taxes this year.
8. Her general expenses of living (food, utilities, etc.) were $15,000 this year.

In calculating her Ḥuqúqu'lláh, she determines that according to the Writings, her residence and needful household furnishings are exempt. Moreover, her car is needful business equipment. Thus, #1, #2, and #3 are exempt in determining the amount of her assets. Jackie's assets do include her stocks, savings account, and her salary. From her $25,000 salary, she must deduct taxes and general expenses of living, which leaves her with $4,000 cash ($25,000 - $6,000 - $15,000).

The basic unit of wealth on which Ḥuqúqu'lláh is payable is nineteen mithqáls of gold. Nineteen mithqáls equals 2.225 troy ounces. If at the present time the value of gold is $400 per ounce, then 19 mithqáls, or 2.225 ounces, of gold is worth $890 ($400 x 2.225). In the chart below, Jackie has described this unit of wealth as "Ḥuqúq Units." The column labelled "Whole Units" indicates the number of whole units on which Ḥuqúq is payable. The "Amount Paid" equals 19% of the value of the "Whole Units."

Date	Item	Value	One Unit	Ḥuqúq Units	Whole Units	Amount Paid
1996	stocks	$2,000 ÷ $890	=	2.25		
	savings	$700 ÷ $890	=	0.79		
	cash	$4,000 ÷ $890	=	4.49		
TOTAL		$6,700 ÷ $890	=	7.53	7	$1,183.70

Jackie has 7.53 units of wealth, but Ḥuqúq is payable only on whole units, so she will pay on 7 units in 1996. Because each unit is worth $890, the value of 7 units is 7 x $890 or $6,230. Jackie must pay 19% of this amount or $1,183.70 (19% x $6,230). Because our possessions are subject only once to the payment of Ḥuqúqu'lláh, she will pay Ḥuqúqu'lláh in the future only on the value of assets when they exceed $6,230. For example, if the next time she calculates Ḥuqúqu'lláh, her assets have increased in value to $8,010, then she will pay Ḥuqúqu'lláh only on the increase of $1,780 ($8,010 - $6,230). Assuming the value of gold is the same, the cash amount of Ḥuqúqu'lláh she would pay would be $338.20 (19% x $1,780).

116

The above procedure presents only one method of calculation. As always, what is important is not the procedure but the principles and the spirit which underlie the law of Ḥuqúqu'lláh. The Bahá'í who studies the Writings on the subject of Ḥuqúqu'lláh will work out methods he or she finds suitable.

Addresses for the Bahá'í Ḥuqúqu'lláh Trust

In the United States, payments of Ḥuqúqu'lláh should be directed to "The Bahá'í Ḥuqúqu'lláh Trust" and sent to one of the following Trustees, who forward payments to the Universal House of Justice.

Dr. Amin Banani
2320 Alta Avenue
Santa Monica, CA 90402

Mr. Stephen Birkland
1192 Benton Way
Arden Hills, MN 55112

Dr. Daryush Haghighi
21300 Avalon Drive
Rocky River, OH 44116

Note: The above names and addresses are current as of 1998. Names and addresses of Trustees are regularly published in *The American Bahá'í* newspaper.

Addresses for the Bahá'í Funds

In the United States, contributions for the International Fund, the Continental Fund, the National Fund, and the Arc Projects Fund may be earmarked and sent to:

c/o National Bahá'í Fund
Wilmette, IL 60091

Contact your Local Spiritual Assembly in regard to whom Local Fund contributions should be remitted.

Appendix F

Holy Days and the Nineteen Day Feast

Bahá'í Holy Days

"He [the Guardian] wishes also to stress the fact that, according to our Bahá'í laws, work is forbidden on our nine holy days. Believers who have independent businesses or shops should refrain from working on these days. Those who are in government employ should, on religious grounds, make an effort to be excused from work; all believers, whoever their employers, should do likewise. If the government, or other employers, refuse to grant them these days off, they are not required to forfeit their employment, but they should make every effort to have the independent status of their Faith recognized and their right to hold their own religious holy days acknowledged."[283]

The following is a listing of Bahá'í holy days on which work and school are suspended. In addition, Bahá'í communities gather together to commemorate these holy days.

March 21   Naw-Rúz [pronounced "No-rooz"]—celebrates the Bahá'í New Year. In one His prayers, Bahá'u'lláh states that God "hast ordained Naw-Rúz as a festival unto those who have observed the fast for love of Thee and abstained from all that is abhorrent unto Thee."[284]

April 21   First Day of Riḍván [pronounced "Rez-von"]

April 29   Ninth Day of Riḍván

119

May 2	Twelfth Day of Riḍván—These three days celebrate the declaration, in the Garden of Riḍván in Baghdad during twelve days in 1863, of Bahá'u'lláh's prophetic mission. Riḍván is "the holiest and most significant of all Bahá'í festivals"[285] and is referred to by Bahá'u'lláh as "the King of Festivals." Although the festival runs for twelve days, from April 21st till May 2nd, work and school are suspended only on the first, ninth, and twelfth days of Riḍván.
May 23	Declaration of the Báb—celebrates the day the Báb declared His mission to Mullá Ḥusayn in 1844, signalizing the beginning of the Bahá'í Era.
May 29	Ascension of Bahá'u'lláh—commemorates the passing of Bahá'u'lláh in 1892.
July 9	Martyrdom of the Báb—commemorates the martyrdom of the Báb in 1850.
October 20	Birth of the Báb—celebrates the Báb's birth in 1819.
November 12	Birth of Bahá'u'lláh—celebrates Bahá'u'lláh's birth in 1817.

The following are also Bahá'í holy days that are commemorated; however, work and school are *not* suspended on these days:

November 26	Day of the Covenant—celebrates the appointment by Bahá'u'lláh of the Center of the Covenant ('Abdu'l-Bahá).
November 28	Ascension of 'Abdu'l-Bahá—commemorates the passing of 'Abdu'l-Bahá in 1921.

Nineteen Day Feast

The following is a listing of the months of the Bahá'í calendar. The Nineteen Day Feast is typically held on the first day of the month.

MONTH	NAME OF MONTH (ENGLISH/ARABIC)	FIRST DAY
1st	Splendor/Bahá	March 21
2nd	Glory/Jalál	April 9
3rd	Beauty/Jamál	April 28
4th	Grandeur/'Aẓamat	May 17
5th	Light/Núr	June 5
6th	Mercy/Raḥmat	June 24
7th	Words/Kalimát	July 13
8th	Perfection/Kamál	August 1
9th	Names/Asmá'	August 20
10th	Might/'Izzat	September 8
11th	Will/Mashíyyat	September 27
12th	Knowledge/'Ilm	October 16
13th	Power/Qudrat	November 4
14th	Speech/Qawl	November 23
15th	Questions/Masá'il	December 12
16th	Honor/Sharaf	December 31
17th	Sovereignty/Sulṭán	January 19
18th	Dominion/Mulk	February 7
19th	Loftiness/'Alá'	March 2

Other Significant Days

It should be noted that the period of the Fast begins on March 2nd of each year and ends March 20th. The Fast is preceded by certain days of festivities, known as the Intercalary Days, or Ayyám-i-Há, which extend from February 26th through March 1st. Bahá'u'lláh has written about the Intercalary Days: "It behoveth the people of Bahá, throughout these days, to provide good cheer for themselves, their kindred and, beyond them, the poor and needy, and with joy and exultation to hail and glorify their Lord, to sing His praise and magnify His Name; and when they end—these days of giving that precede the season of re-

121

straint—let them enter upon the Fast."[286] Bahá'ís celebrate these days through hospitality, charity, and gift-giving.

Appendix G

Study Questions and Exercises

Introduction

Study Questions

1. What are the two natures in man? Each nature tends towards what?

2. God chose to confer upon man what unique distinction and capacity?

3. What should be the ultimate aim in life of every soul?

4. "Men who suffer not, attain no _____."

5. What is the potent instrument by which individual belief in Bahá'u'lláh is translated into constructive deeds?

6. The Twin Successors of Bahá'u'lláh and 'Abdu'l-Bahá are _____ and _____.

7. 'Abdu'l-Bahá's life and deeds were the inevitable and spontaneous expression of what?

8. "The universal crisis affecting mankind is . . . essentially _____ in its causes."

9. The chief goal of the Bahá'í Faith is the development of the individual and society through what means?

10. List the essential requisites for our spiritual growth.

Memorization Exercises

1. "Having created the world and all that liveth and moveth therein, He, through the direct operation of His unconstrained and sovereign Will, chose to confer upon man the unique distinction and capacity to know Him and to love Him. . . . Upon the inmost reality of each and every created thing He hath shed the light of one of His names, and made it a recipient of the glory of one of His attributes. Upon the reality of man, however, He hath focused the radiance of all of His names and attributes, and made it a mirror of His own Self."

(Gleanings from the Writings of Bahá'u'lláh, p. 65)

2. "When a person becomes a Bahá'í, actually what takes place is that the seed of the spirit starts to grow in the human soul. This seed must be watered by the outpourings of the Holy Spirit. These gifts of the spirit are received through prayer, meditation, study of the Holy Utterances and service to the Cause of God."

(On behalf of Shoghi Effendi, *Living the Life,* p. 35)

3. ". . . in the beginning the believers must make their steps firm in the Covenant so that the confirmations of Bahá'u'lláh may encircle them from all sides, the cohorts of the Supreme Concourse may become their supporters and helpers, and the exhortations and advices of 'Abdu'l-Bahá, like unto the pictures engraved on stone, may remain permanent and ineffaceable in the tablets of all hearts."

('Abdu'l-Bahá, *Tablets of the Divine Plan,* p. 52)

Prayer

Study Questions

1. The sense of spirituality can be acquired chiefly by what means?

2. According to 'Abdu'l-Bahá, obligatory prayers are conducive to what?

3. What are the definitions of "morning," "noon," and "evening" in relation to the three Obligatory Prayers?

4. What is the significance of turning toward the Shrine of Bahá'u'lláh when saying the obligatory prayer?

5. What are the exemptions for the Obligatory Prayers?

6. Ablutions consist of what?

7. To whom should we turn our thoughts to in prayer?

8. For what should we pray?

9. Prayer can only be answered through what?

10. What is the significance of the words and movements of the obligatory prayer?

Memorization Exercises

1. "The obligatory prayers are binding inasmuch as they are conducive to humility and submissiveness, to setting one's face toward God and expressing devotion to Him. Through such prayer man holdeth communion with God, seeketh to draw near unto Him, converseth with the true Beloved of one's heart, and attaineth spiritual stations."

('Abdu'l-Bahá, *Spiritual Foundations* #23)

2. "Know thou that in every word and movement of the obligatory prayer there are allusions, mysteries and a wisdom that man is unable to comprehend, and letters and scrolls cannot contain."

('Abdu'l-Bahá, *Spiritual Foundations* #27)

3. "The most acceptable prayer is the one offered with the utmost spirituality and radiance; its prolongation hath not been and is not beloved by God. The more detached and the purer the prayer, the more acceptable is it in the presence of God."

(*Selections from the Writings of the Báb*, p. 78)

Reciting the Verses of God and Meditation

Study Questions

1. When must we recite the verses of God?

2. What is the definition of "verses of God"?

3. How does the practice of reciting the verses of God differ from study of the Faith?

4. In what spirit should the verses be recited?

5. What is the definition of meditation? How does 'Abdu'l-Bahá describe meditation?

6. When are the results of meditation confirmed?

7. Whose words should we use when meditating?

8. Is there a set form of meditation prescribed in the Teachings?

9. What are the consequences of failing to recite the verses of God every morning and evening?

10. What are the effects when a person, in the privacy of his chamber, recites the verses revealed by God?

Memorization Exercises

1. "Recite ye the verses of God every morn and eventide. Whoso faileth to recite them hath not been faithful to the Covenant of God and His Testament, and whoso turneth away from these holy verses in this Day is of those who throughout eternity have turned away from God."

(Bahá'u'lláh, *Kitáb-i-Aqdas*, parag. 149)

2. "It behoveth us one and all to recite day and night both the Persian and Arabic *Hidden Words*, to pray fervently and supplicate tearfully that we may be enabled to conduct ourselves in accordance with these di-

vine counsels. These holy Words have not been revealed to be heard but to be practiced." ('Abdu'l-Bahá, *Deepening #37*)

3. "Be assured in thyself that if thou dost conduct thyself in accordance with the *Hidden Words* revealed in Persian and in Arabic, thou shalt become a torch of fire of the love of God, an embodiment of humility, of lowliness, of evanescence and of selflessness."

('Abdu'l-Bahá, *Deepening #39*)

4. "Were any man to ponder in his heart that which the Pen of the Most High hath revealed and to taste of its sweetness, he would, of a certainty, find himself emptied and delivered from his own desires, and utterly subservient to the Will of the Almighty. Happy is the man that hath attained so high a station, and hath not deprived himself of so bountiful a grace." (*Gleanings from the Writings of Bahá'u'lláh*, p. 343)

Study of the Faith

Study Questions

1. What must remain the first obligation and the object of the constant endeavor of every Bahá'í?

2. What is primarily meant by deepening?

3. Is the understanding and comprehension of the Words of God dependent upon human learning? If not, upon what do they depend?

4. What are the twofold and sacred obligations of every responsible and active follower of the Faith?

5. The Universal House of Justice has explained that study of the Faith includes what?

6. What make up the Sacred Scriptures of the Faith? What make up the authoritative Writings of the Faith?

7. What are some of the books and subjects we should study?

8. What can just one mature soul, with spiritual understanding and a profound knowledge of the Faith, achieve?

9. Young Bahá'ís should gain a mastery of what books?

10. What is the definition of a Bahá'í scholar?

Memorization Exercises

1. "My holy, My divinely ordained Revelation may be likened unto an ocean in whose depths are concealed innumerable pearls of great price, of surpassing luster. It is the duty of every seeker to bestir himself and strive to attain the shores of this ocean, so that he may, in proportion to the eagerness of his search and the efforts he hath exerted, partake of such benefits as have been preordained in God's irrevocable and hidden Tablets. If no one be willing to direct his steps towards its shores, if every one should fail to arise and find Him, can such a failure be said to have robbed this ocean of its power or to have lessened, to any degree, its treasures?" *(Gleanings from the Writings of Bahá'u'lláh, p. 326)*

2. "In this day there is nothing more important than the instruction and study of clear proofs and convincing, heavenly arguments, for therein lie the source of life and the path of salvation."

('Abdu'l-Bahá, *Deepening* #31)

3. "Indeed if an avowed follower of Bahá'u'lláh were to immerse himself in, and fathom the depths of, the ocean of these heavenly teachings, and with utmost care and attention deduce from each of them the subtle mysteries and consummate wisdom that lie enshrined therein, such a person's life, materially, intellectually and spiritually, will be safe from toil and trouble, and unaffected by setbacks and perils, or any sadness or despondency." (Shoghi Effendi, *Deepening* #69)

Teaching the Faith

Study Questions

1. Should the work of teaching lapse, what will be the spiritual consequences?

2. What are some of the spiritual qualities that 'Abdu'l-Bahá states the teacher must possess?

3. What attracts God's blessings and enables us to become more fitted for serving the Faith?

4. What are some of the specific actions that the Writings state the teacher should take?

5. Whom should we teach?

6. What is the most effective way to teach?

7. When we teach, what should we say?

8. How often, at a minimum, should Bahá'ís have teaching gatherings in their homes?

9. What makes one a "best teacher" and an "exemplary believer"?

10. Is the purpose of teaching complete when a person declares that he has accepted Bahá'u'lláh?

Memorization Exercises

1. "Teach ye the Cause of God, O people of Bahá, for God hath prescribed unto every one the duty of proclaiming His Message, and regardeth it as the most meritorious of all deeds."

(Gleanings from the Writings of Bahá'u'lláh, p. 278)

2. "The aim is this: The intention of the teacher must be pure, his heart independent, his spirit attracted, his thought at peace, his resolution

129

firm, his magnanimity exalted and in the love of God a shining torch. Should he become as such, his sanctified breath will even affect the rock; otherwise there will be no result whatsoever. As long as a soul is not perfected, how can he efface the defects of others?"

('Abdu'l-Bahá, *Tablets of the Divine Plan*, p. 54)

3. "In these days, the most important of all things is the guidance of the nations and peoples of the world. Teaching the Cause is of utmost importance for it is the head cornerstone of the foundation itself. This wronged servant has spent his days and nights in promoting the Cause and urging the peoples to service. He rested not a moment, till the fame of the Cause of God was noised abroad in the world and the celestial strains from the Abhá Kingdom roused the East and the West. The beloved of God must also follow the same example. This is the secret of faithfulness, this is the requirement of servitude to the Threshold of Bahá!"

(*Will and Testament of 'Abdu'l-Bahá*, p. 10)

Observance of Divine Laws and Principles

Study Questions

1. What are the twin duties of man?

2. Can man's knowledge of God develop without observing what God has revealed?

3. What law occupies "an exalted station in the sight of God"?

4. What is the significance of fasting?

5. What are the exemptions for fasting?

6. Name some basic Bahá'í laws.

7. What are the effects of backbiting?

8. How can we remain steadfast in the Cause of God?

9. What will be the effects of our obedience to the laws of God?

10. What are the blessings connected with the *Kitáb-i-Aqdas*?

Memorization Exercises

1. "The first duty prescribed by God for His servants is the recognition of Him Who is the Dayspring of His Revelation and the Fountain of His laws, Who representeth the Godhead in both the Kingdom of His Cause and the world of creation. Whoso achieveth this duty hath attained unto all good; and whoso is deprived thereof hath gone astray, though he be the author of every righteous deed. It behoveth every one who reacheth this most sublime station, this summit of transcendent glory, to observe every ordinance of Him Who is the Desire of the world. These twin duties are inseparable. Neither is acceptable without the other." (Bahá'u'lláh, *Kitáb-i-Aqdas*, parag. 1)

2. "Know assuredly that My commandments are the lamps of My loving providence among My servants, and the keys of My mercy for My creatures." (Bahá'u'lláh, *Kitáb-i-Aqdas*, parag. 3)

3. "The purpose of the one true God in manifesting Himself is to summon all mankind to truthfulness and sincerity, to piety and trustworthiness, to resignation and submissiveness to the Will of God, to forbearance and kindliness, to uprightness and wisdom. His object is to array every man with the mantle of a saintly character, and to adorn him with the ornament of holy and goodly deeds." (*Gleanings from the Writings of Bahá'u'lláh*, p. 299)

Ḥuqúqu'lláh and the Bahá'í Funds

Study Questions

1. At all times one must have the utmost regard for what?

2. What are the two types of material offerings in the Faith?

3. What is the law of Ḥuqúqu'lláh?

4. What are the purposes and effects of the law of Huqúqu'lláh?

5. What are blessings of the law of Ḥuqúqu'lláh?

6. In what spirit should Ḥuqúqu'lláh be offered?

7. In contributing to the Fund, what will be the cause of attracting spiritual confirmations?

8. What are the four major Funds?

9. What are the differences between Ḥuqúqu'lláh and the Funds?

10. Why is it important to contribute to the Arc Projects Fund?

Memorization Exercises

1. "Should anyone acquire one hundred mithqáls of gold, nineteen mithqáls thereof are God's and to be rendered unto Him, the Fashioner of earth and heaven. Take heed, O people, lest ye deprive yourselves of so great a bounty. This We have commanded you, though We are well able to dispense with you and with all who are in the heavens and on earth; in it there are benefits and wisdoms beyond the ken of anyone but God, the Omniscient, the All-Informed."

(Bahá'u'lláh, *Kitáb-i-Aqdas*, parag. 97)

2. "Ḥuqúqu'lláh is indeed a great law. It is incumbent upon all to make this offering, because it is the source of grace, abundance, and of all good. It is a bounty which shall remain with every soul in every world of the worlds of God, the All-Possessing, the All-Bountiful."

(Bahá'u'lláh, *Ḥuqúqu'lláh* #7)

3. "The overwhelming majority of the Bahá'ís in the world are poor people, but it is to the believers, and to the believers alone, that Bahá'u'lláh has given the bounty of contributing the material things of this world for the progress of His Faith. It is not the amount of the contribution which is important, but the degree of self-sacrifice that it entails—for it is this that attracts the confirmations of God."

(Universal House of Justice, *Lights of Guidance*, p. 250)

132

Service

Study Questions

1. Service takes what forms?

2. How did 'Abdu'l-Bahá view His own station?

3. What is the spiritual significance of selflessly pursuing one's profession?

4. Is it a service to God to acquire knowledge of the arts and sciences and learn a trade or profession?

5. With what attitude should we enter the Nineteen Day Feast?

6. In Bahá'í elections, we should vote for those who can best combine what necessary qualities?

7. What are the first and second conditions of consultation?

8. Those who consult must proceed in what manner?

9. In order to live the Teachings of the Faith, is it necessary to be active with the Bahá'í community?

10. What are the prime requisites for those who consult?

Memorization Exercises

1. "Think ye at all times of rendering some service to every member of the human race. Pay ye no heed to aversion and rejection, to disdain, hostility, injustice: act ye in the opposite way. Be ye sincerely kind, not in appearance only. Let each one of God's loved ones centre his attention on this: to be the Lord's mercy to man; to be the Lord's grace. Let him do some good to every person whose path he crosseth, and be of some benefit to him. Let him improve the character of each and all, and reorient the minds of men."

(*Selections from the Writings of 'Abdu'l-Bahá*, p. 3)

2. "There is nothing that brings success in the Faith like service. Service is the magnet which draws the divine confirmations. Thus, when a person is active, they are blessed by the Holy Spirit. When they are inactive, the Holy Spirit cannot find a repository in their being, and thus they are deprived of its healing and quickening rays."

(On behalf of Shoghi Effendi, *Living the Life*, p. 34)

3. "The prime requisites for them that take counsel together are purity of motive, radiance of spirit, detachment from all else save God, attraction to His Divine Fragrances, humility and lowliness amongst His loved ones, patience and long-suffering in difficulties and servitude to His exalted Threshold. Should they be graciously aided to acquire these attributes, victory from the unseen Kingdom of Bahá shall be vouchsafed to them."

('Abdu'l-Bahá, *Consultation #9*)

Bibliography

Works by the Authoritative Centers of the Faith
'Abdu'l-Bahá.

———*'Abdu'l-Bahá in London.* London: Bahá'í Publishing Trust, 1987.
———*Memorials of the Faithful.* Wilmette, IL: Bahá'í Publishing Trust, 1975.
———*Paris Talks.* London: Bahá'í Publishing Trust, 1961 (10th ed).
———*Promulgation of Universal Peace.* Wilmette, IL: Bahá'í Publishing Trust, 1982.
———*Secret of Divine Civilization.* Wilmette, IL: Bahá'í Publishing Trust, 1990.
———*Selections from the Writings of 'Abdu'l-Bahá.* Haifa: Bahá'í World Centre, 1982.
———*Some Answered Questions.* Wilmette, IL: Bahá'í Publishing Trust, 1990.
———*Tablets of the Divine Plan.* Wilmette, IL: Bahá'í Publishing Trust, 1993.
———*A Traveller's Narrative.* Wilmette, IL: Bahá'í Publishing Trust, 1980.
———*Will and Testament of 'Abdu'l-Bahá.* Wilmette, IL: Bahá'í Publishing Trust, 1990.

The Báb.

———*Selections from the Writings of the Báb.* Haifa: Bahá'í World Centre, 1982.

Bahá'u'lláh.

———*Epistle to the Son of the Wolf.* Wilmette, IL: Bahá'í Publishing Trust, 1988.
———*Gleanings from the Writings of Bahá'u'lláh.* Wilmette, IL: Bahá'í Publishing Trust, 1983.
———*Hidden Words.* Wilmette, IL: Bahá'í Publishing Trust, 1990.
———*Kitáb-i-Aqdas: The Most Holy Book.* Haifa: Bahá'í World Centre, 1992.
———*Kitáb-i-Íqán: The Book of Certitude.* Wilmette, IL: Bahá'í Publishing Trust, 1989.
———*Prayers and Meditations.* Wilmette, IL: Bahá'í Publishing Trust, 1987.
———*Proclamation of Bahá'u'lláh.* Haifa: Bahá'í World Centre, 1972.
———*Seven Valleys and the Four Valleys.* Wilmette, IL: Bahá'í Publishing Trust, 1991.
———*Tablets of Bahá'u'lláh.* Wilmette, IL: Bahá'í Publishing Trust, 1988.

Shoghi Effendi.

————*Advent of Divine Justice*. Wilmette, IL: Bahá'í Publishing Trust, 1984.

————*Arohanui: Letters from Shoghi Effendi to New Zealand*. Fiji Islands: Bahá'í Publishing Trust, 1982.

————*Bahá'í Administration*. Wilmette, IL: Bahá'í Publishing Trust, 1968.

————*Citadel of Faith*. Wilmette, IL: Bahá'í Publishing Trust, 1965.

————*Dawn-Breakers: Nabíl's Narrative of the Early Days of the Bahá'í Revelation*. New York: Bahá'í Publishing Committee, 1953.

————*God Passes By*. Wilmette, IL: Bahá'í Publishing Trust, 1979 (rev. ed.).

————*High Endeavours: Messages to Alaska*. Anchorage, Alaska: National Spiritual Assembly of the Bahá'ís of Alaska, 1976.

————*Japan Will Turn Ablaze!* Japan: Bahá'í Publishing Trust of Japan, 1992 (rev. ed.).

————*Light of Divine Guidance (Vol. I)*. Hofheim-Langenhain, Germany: Bahá'í-Verlag, 1982.

————*Light of Divine Guidance (Vol. II)*. Hofheim-Langenhain, Germany: Bahá'í-Verlag, 1985.

————*Messages to America: 1932-46*. Wilmette, IL: Bahá'í Publishing Committee, 1947.

————*Messages to the Antipodes*. New South Wales, Australia: Bahá'í Publications Australia, 1997.

————*Messages to Canada*. Canada: National Spiritual Assembly of the Bahá'ís of Canada, 1965.

————*Messages to the Bahá'í World: 1950-57*. Wilmette, IL: Bahá'í Publishing Trust, 1971.

————*Messages of Shoghi Effendi to the Indian Subcontinent: 1923-1957*. New Delhi, India: Bahá'i Publishing Trust, 1995 (rev. ed.).

————*Promised Day Is Come*. Wilmette, IL: Bahá'í Publishing Trust, 1980 (rev. ed.).

————*Unfolding Destiny*. London: Bahá'í Publishing Trust, 1981.

————*World Order of Bahá'u'lláh*. Wilmette, IL: Bahá'í Publishing Trust, 1982.

Universal House of Justice.

————*Constitution of the Universal House of Justice*. Haifa: Bahá'í World Centre, 1972.

————*Four Year Plan: Messages of the Universal House of Justice*. Riviera Beach, FL: Palabra Publications, 1996.

————*Holy Year: 1992-1993*. Riviera Beach, FL: Palabra Publications, 1993.

————*Individual Rights and Freedoms in the World Order of Bahá'u'lláh*. Wilmette, IL: Bahá'í Publishing Trust, 1989.

————*Messages from the Universal House of Justice: 1963-1986*. Wilmette, IL: Bahá'í Publishing Trust, 1996.

————*Messages from the Universal House of Justice: 1968-1973*. Wilmette, IL: Bahá'í Publishing Trust, 1976.

————*Promise of World Peace.* Wilmette, IL: Bahá'í Publishing Trust, 1985.

————*Rights & Responsibilities.* Thornhill, Ontario: Bahá'i Publications Canada, 1997.

————Unpublished letter (on behalf of the Universal House of Justice) dated June 5, 1988, to an individual believer.

————November 26, 1992, to the Bahá'ís of the World.

————Unpublished letter dated March 5, 1993, to the Bahá'ís of the World.

————Ridván 150 (1993), to the Bahá'ís of the World.

————Unpublished letter dated June 24, 1993, to the Bahá'ís of the World.

————Unpublished letter dated January 4, 1994, to all National Spiritual Assemblies.

————Ridván 151 (1994), to the Bahá'ís of the World.

————May 19, 1994, to the National Spiritual Assembly of the Bahá'ís of United States.

————Unpublished letter (on behalf of the Universal House of Justice) dated November 30, 1995, to an individual believer.

————*Wellspring of Guidance: 1963-1968.* Wilmette, IL: Bahá'í Publishing Trust, 1976 (rev. ed.).

————*A Wider Horizon: 1983-1992.* Riviera Beach, FL: Palabra Publications, 1992.

Compilations

————*Bahá'í Education.* London: Bahá'í Publishing Trust, 1987 (rev. ed).

————*Bahá'í Elections.* London: Bahá'í Publishing Trust, 1990.

————*Bahá'í Funds: Contributions and Administration.* Thornhill, Ontario: Bahá'í Canada Publications, 1988.

————*Bahá'í Meetings/The Nineteen Day Feast.* Wilmette, IL: Bahá'í Publishing Trust, 1976.

————*Bahá'í World Faith.* Wilmette, IL: Bahá'í Publishing Trust, 1956 (2d ed.).

————*Bahá'í Writings on Music.* Oakham, England: Bahá'í Publishing Trust, n.d.

————*Bahíyyíh Khánum.* Haifa: Bahá'í World Centre, 1982.

————*Centres of Bahá'í Learning.* Wilmette, IL: Bahá'í Publishing Trust, 1980.

————*Chaste and Holy Life.* London: Bahá'í Publishing Trust, 1988.

————*Compilation of Compilations (Vol. I, II).* Victoria, Australia: Bahá'í Publications Australia, 1991.

————*Conservation of the Earth's Resources.* London: Bahá'í Publishing Trust, 1990.

————*Consultation.* London: Bahá'í Publishing Trust, 1990 (rev. ed.).

————*Covenant.* London: Bahá'í Publishing Trust, 1988.

————*Crisis and Victory.* London: Bahá'í Publishing Trust, 1988.

————*Divorce.* Oakham, England: Bahá'í Publishing Trust, 1986.

————*Entry by Troops.* New South Wales, Australia: Bahá'í Publications Australia, 1994.

―――Excellence in All Things. London: Bahá'í Publishing Trust, 1989 (rev. ed).

―――Family Life. Oakham, England: Bahá'í Publishing Trust, 1982.

―――Health and Healing. New Delhi, India: Bahá'í Publishing Trust, 1994.

―――Ḥuqúqu'lláh. Thornhill, Ontario: Bahá'í Canada Publications, 1986.

―――Ḥuqúqu'lláh: A Study Guide. London: Bahá'í Publishing Trust, 1989.

―――Importance of Deepening our Knowledge and Understanding of the Faith. Ontario, Canada: Bahá'í Community of Canada, 1983.

―――Individual and Teaching. Thornhill, Ontario: Bahá'í Community of Canada, 1977.

―――Lights of Guidance: A Bahá'í Reference File. Helen Hornby, ed. New Delhi, India: Bahá'í Publishing Trust, 1988 (2d rev. ed.).

―――Living the Life. London: Bahá'í Publishing Trust, 1974.

―――Local Spiritual Assembly. Wilmette, IL: Bahá'í Publishing Trust, n.d.

―――National Convention. New South Wales, Australia: Bahá'í Publications Australia, 1993.

―――National Spiritual Assembly. Oakham, England: Bahá'í Publishing Trust, 1973 (2d ed).

―――Peace. London: Bahá'í Publishing Trust, 1985.

―――Power of Divine Assistance. Oakham, England: Bahá'í Publishing Trust, 1981.

―――Preserving Bahá'í Marriages. Thornhill, Ontario: Bahá'í Canada Publications, 1991.

―――A Special Measure of Love: The Importance and Nature of the Teaching Work among the Masses. Wilmette, IL: Bahá'í Publishing Trust, 1974.

―――Spiritual Foundations: Prayer, Meditation, and the Devotional Attitude. Ontario, Canada: Bahá'í Community of Canada, 1980.

―――Stirring of the Spirit: Celebrating the Institution of the Nineteen Day Feast. Thornhill, Ontario: Bahá'í Canada Publications, 1990.

―――Teaching Prominent People. London: Bahá'í Publishing Trust, 1990.

―――Trustworthiness. London: Bahá'í Publishing Trust, 1987.

―――Universal House of Justice. Oakham, England: Bahá'í Publishing Trust, 1984.

―――Women. Oakham, England: Bahá'í Publishing Trust, 1986.

―――Youth. Wilmette, IL: Bahá'í Publishing Trust, 1973.

Other Sources

H.M. Balyuzi. 'Abdu'l-Bahá: The Centre of the Covenant of Bahá'u'lláh. Oxford: George Ronald, 1987.

Bahá'í Prayers. Wilmette, IL: Bahá'í Publishing Trust, 1991.

Bahá'u'lláh's Teachings on Spirituality Reality. Riviera Beach, FL: Palabra Publications, 1996.

Covenant: Its Meaning and Origin and Our Attitude Toward It. National Spiritual Assembly of the Bahá'ís of the United States, 1988.

Honnold, Annamarie (ed.). *Vignettes from the Life of 'Abdu'l-Bahá*. Oxford: George Ronald, 1986.

Ives, Howard Colby. *Portals to Freedom*. Oxford: George Ronald, 1953.

Maxwell, May. *An Early Pilgrimage*. Oxford: George Ronald, 1976.

Moffett, Ruth J. *Du'á: On Wings of Prayer*. Naturegraph Publishers, 1984.

Proofs of Bahá'u'lláh's Mission. Riviera Beach, FL: Palabra Publications, 1994.

Rabbaní, Rúhíyyih. *Priceless Pearl*. London: Bahá'í Publishing Trust, 1969.

Reciting the Verses of God: Spiritual Virtues and Practices. New Delhi, India: Bahá'í Publishing Trust, 1995.

Smith, Melanie Sarachman and William Diehl. *Reading Bahá'u'lláh's Word*. Riviera Beach, FL: Palabra Publications, 1997.

Sobhani, Mohi (trans.). *Maḥmúd's Diary*. Oxford: George Ronald, 1998.

Spiritual Conquest of the Planet. Riviera Beach, FL: Palabra Publications, 1993.

Vafai, Shahin. *Raising The Call: The Individual and Effective Teaching*. Riviera Beach, FL: Palabra Publications, 1998.

"Vineyard of the Lord," No. 14, March 1996.

Word of God. National Spiritual Assembly of the Bahá'ís of the United States, 1987.

References

1. *Kitáb-i-Íqán*, p. 120.
2. *Some Answered Questions*, p. 118.
3. *Selections from the Writings of 'Abdu'l-Bahá*, p. 288.
4. *The Promulgation of Universal Peace*, p. 41.
5. *Gleanings from the Writings of Bahá'u'lláh*, p. 65.
6. *Gleanings from the Writings of Bahá'u'lláh*, p. 65.
7. *Selections from the Writings of 'Abdu'l-Bahá*, p. 140.
8. *The Promulgation of Universal Peace*, p. 70.
9. *Messages from the Universal House of Justice: 1963-1986*, p. 377.
10. *The Promulgation of Universal Peace*, p. 166.
11. On behalf of the Universal House of Justice, *Lights of Guidance*, pp. 540-41.
12. *Gleanings from the Writings of Bahá'u'lláh*, p. 143.
13. On behalf of Shoghi Effendi, *Living the Life*, p. 10.
14. *Hidden Words*, Arabic #50.
15. *Paris Talks*, p. 51.
16. *Hidden Words*, Arabic #31.
17. *Tablets of Bahá'u'lláh*, p. 138.
18. On behalf of Shoghi Effendi, *Spiritual Foundations: Prayer, Meditation, and the Devotional Attitude* [hereinafter *Spiritual Foundations*] #51.
19. *Individual Rights and Freedoms in the World Order of Bahá'u'lláh*, p. 5.
20. See *Individual Rights and Freedoms in the World Order of Bahá'u'lláh*, p. 5.
21. *See* Universal House of Justice, message dated November 26, 1992, to the Bahá'ís of the World.
22. Universal House of Justice, quoted in *The Covenant*, Introduction.
23. Universal House of Justice, *Kitáb-i-Aqdas*, Introduction, p. 3.
24. *Individual Rights and Freedoms in the World Order of Bahá'u'lláh*, p. 5.
25. Universal House of Justice, message dated November 26, 1992, to the Bahá'ís of the World.
26. See *The World Order of Bahá'u'lláh*, p. 134.
27. *Messages from the Universal House of Justice (1968-1973)*, p. 25.
28. *Hidden Words*, Arabic #16.
29. On behalf of Shoghi Effendi, *Spiritual Foundations* #40.

30. On behalf ot Shoghi Effendi, *Spiritual Foundations* #40.

31. On behalf of Shoghi Effendi, *Spiritual Foundations* #52.

32. 'Abdu'l-Bahá, quoted in letter on behalf of the Universal House of Justice, *Lights of Guidance*, p. 541.

33. *Kitáb-i-Aqdas*, parag. 10.

34. *Kitáb-i-Aqdas*, Questions and Answers #93.

35. 'Abdu'l-Bahá, *Spiritual Foundations* #23.

36. 'Abdu'l-Bahá, *Spiritual Foundations* #23.

37. *Prayers and Meditations*, p. 314.

38. See *Kitáb-i-Aqdas*, Note #5.

39. *Prayers and Meditations*, p. 316.

40. See *Kitáb-i-Aqdas*, Note #5.

41. See *Prayers and Meditations*, p. 323.

42. On behalf of Shoghi Effendi, *Spiritual Foundations* #59.

43. See *Kitáb-i-Aqdas*, Note #13.

44. See *Kitáb-i-Aqdas*, Note #14.

45. *Kitáb-i-Aqdas*, Questions and Answers #93.

46. *Kitáb-i-Aqdas*, Note #21.

47. *Kitáb-i-Aqdas*, Questions and Answers #58.

48. On behalf of the Universal House of Justice, *Lights of Guidance*, p. 541.

49. See *Kitáb-i-Aqdas*, Note #19.

50. *Kitáb-i-Aqdas*, Note #19.

51. *Kitáb-i-Aqdas*, Note #19.

52. *Kitáb-i-Aqdas*, Note #34.

53. *Kitáb-i-Aqdas*, Note #34.

54. *Kitáb-i-Aqdas*, Note #4.

55. On behalf of Shoghi Effendi, *Spiritual Foundations* #48.

56. On behalf of the Universal House of Justice, *Lights of Guidance*, p. 542.

57. See *Kitáb-i-Aqdas*, Note #19.

58. On behalf of Shoghi Effendi, *Spiritual Foundations* #43.

59. On behalf of Shoghi Effendi, *Spiritual Foundations* #44.

60. See on behalf of Shoghi Effendi, *Spiritual Foundations* #58.

61. On behalf of Shoghi Effendi, *Spiritual Foundations* #47.

62. On behalf of Shoghi Effendi, *Unfolding Destiny*, p. 154.

63. On behalf of Shoghi Effendi, *Unfolding Destiny*, p. 154.

64. *Prayers and Meditations*, p. 130.

65. *The Promulgation of Universal Peace*, p. 247.

66. *The Promulgation of Universal Peace*, p. 247.

67. On behalf of Shoghi Effendi, *Lights of Guidance*, p. 461.

68. Bahá'u'lláh, *The Importance of Deepening our Knowledge and Understanding of the Faith* [hereinafter *Deepening*] #5.

69. *Kitáb-i-Aqdas*, parag. 149.

70. *Kitáb-i-Aqdas*, Note #165.

71. *See Kitáb-i-Aqdas*, Note #165.
72. On behalf of the Universal House of Justice, message dated November 30, 1995, to an individual believer.
73. *See* Universal House of Justice, letter dated June 24, 1993, to the Bahá'ís of the World.
74. *Kitáb-i-Aqdas*, Questions and Answers #68.
75. *Kitáb-i-Aqdas*, parag. 149.
76. On behalf of the Universal House of Justice, *Lights of Guidance*, p. 540.
77. *Kitáb-i-Aqdas*, parag. 149.
78. *See* Universal House of Justice, *Lights of Guidance*, p. 224.
79. *Paris Talks*, p. 174.
80. *Paris Talks*, p. 175.
81. *Paris Talks*, pp. 175-76.
82. On behalf of Shoghi Effendi, *Spiritual Foundations* #50.
83. *See Paris Talks*, p. 176.
84. *See* on behalf of Shoghi Effendi, *Spiritual Foundations* #39, 61.
85. On behalf of the Universal House of Justice, *Lights of Guidance*, p. 541.
86. On behalf of Shoghi Effendi, *Spiritual Foundations* #50.
87. On behalf of the Universal House of Justice, *Lights of Guidance*, p. 541.
88. On behalf of Shoghi Effendi, *Deepening* #149.
89. *Kitáb-i-Aqdas*, parag. 182.
90. *The World Order of Bahá'u'lláh*, p. 100.
91. *Wellspring of Guidance*, p. 113.
92. 'Abdu'l-Bahá, *Deepening* #27.
93. Bahá'u'lláh, *Deepening* #7.
94. 'Abdu'l-Bahá, *Deepening* #31.
95. *Kitáb-i-Íqán*, p. 211.
96. 'Abdu'l-Bahá, *Deepening* #28.
97. *See* on behalf of the Universal House of Justice, *Lights of Guidance*, p. 540.
98. On behalf of Shoghi Effendi, *Deepening* #115.
99. On behalf of Shoghi Effendi, *The Individual and Teaching* #46.
100. Universal House of Justice, letter dated June 24, 1993, to the Bahá'ís of the World.
101. On behalf of the Universal House of Justice, letter dated June 5, 1988, to an individual believer.
102. On behalf of the Universal House of Justice, letter dated June 5, 1988, to an individual believer.
103. *See* on behalf of Shoghi Effendi, *Lights of Guidance*, p. 439.
104. *See* on behalf of Shoghi Effendi, *Deepening* #102, 106, 109, 123, 126, 127, 129, 143.
105. *The World Order of Bahá'u'lláh*, p. 147.
106. *The World Order of Bahá'u'lláh*, p. 99.
107. *Paris Talks*, p. 22.

108. *Wellspring of Guidance*, p. 114.

109. *The Promulgation of Universal Peace*, p. 459.

110. On behalf of Shoghi Effendi, *Deepening* #153.

111. *Kitáb-i-Aqdas*, parag. 53.

112. *Gleanings from the Writings of Bahá'u'lláh*, p. 278.

113. Bahá'u'lláh, quoted in *The Advent of Divine Justice*, p. 76.

114. *Selections from the Writings of 'Abdu'l-Bahá*, pp. 264-65.

115. *Tablets of the Divine Plan*, p. 54.

116. On behalf of Shoghi Effendi, *The Individual and Teaching* #55.

117. On behalf of Shoghi Effendi, *Lights of Guidance*, p. 599.

118. 'Abdu'l-Bahá, *The Individual and Teaching* #30.

119. See *Tablets of Bahá'u'lláh*, p. 200.

120. *The Advent of Divine Justice*, p. 51.

121. *Gleanings from the Writings of Bahá'u'lláh*, p. 280.

122. 'Abdu'l-Bahá, *The Individual and Teaching* #27.

123. On behalf of Shoghi Effendi, *The Individual and Teaching* #91.

124. *Tablets of Bahá'u'lláh*, p. 200.

125. 'Abdu'l-Bahá, *Deepening* #64.

126. *Selections from the Writings of 'Abdu'l-Bahá*, p. 269.

127. On behalf of Shoghi Effendi, *The Individual and Teaching* #49.

128. Shoghi Effendi, *Arohanui*, p. 28.

129. *Selections from the Writings of the Báb*, p. 77.

130. *Gleanings from the Writings of Bahá'u'lláh*, p. 289.

131. *Gleanings from the Writings of Bahá'u'lláh*, p. 8.

132. On behalf of Shoghi Effendi, *The Individual and Teaching* #109.

133. *Bahá'í Administration*, p. 69.

134. *Will and Testament of 'Abdu'l-Bahá*, p. 10.

135. *Hidden Words*, Arabic #38.

136. *Kitáb-i-Aqdas*, parag. 1.

137. *Kitáb-i-Aqdas*, parag. 1.

138. *Kitáb-i-Aqdas*, parag. 5.

139. *Kitáb-i-Aqdas*, parag. 3.

140. *Tablets of Bahá'u'lláh*, p. 268.

141. *Kitáb-i-Aqdas*, parag. 10.

142. *Kitáb-i-Aqdas*, Questions and Answers #93.

143. *Selections from the Writings of 'Abdu'l-Bahá*, p. 70.

144. See *Kitáb-i-Aqdas*, parag. 17 & Note #25.

145. See *Kitáb-i-Aqdas*, Note #25.

146. See *Kitáb-i-Aqdas*, Note #31.

147. *Prayers and Meditations*, p. 79.

148. Bahá'u'lláh, *Trustworthiness* #1.

149. 'Abdu'l-Bahá, quoted in *The Advent of Divine Justice*, p. 26.

150. *Hidden Words*, Arabic #2.

151. *Kitáb-i-Aqdas*, Questions and Answers #106.

152. *The Four Year Plan: Messages of the Universal House of Justice*, p. 32.

153. Universal House of Justice, letter dated Riḍván 150 (1993), to the Bahá'ís of the World.

154. *Kitáb-i-Íqán*, p. 193.

155. *Kitáb-i-Íqán*, p. 193.

156. *Tablets of Bahá'u'lláh*, p. 51.

157. *Some Answered Questions*, p. 173.

158. *Kitáb-i-Aqdas*, parag. 163.

159. Bahá'u'lláh, *Ḥuqúqu'lláh* #10.

160. Bahá'u'lláh, *Ḥuqúqu'lláh* #1.

161. Bahá'u'lláh, *Ḥuqúqu'lláh* #50.

162. *Kitáb-i-Aqdas*, Note #125.

163. *Kitáb-i-Aqdas*, parag. 97.

164. *Will and Testament of 'Abdu'l-Bahá*, p. 15.

165. Bahá'u'lláh, *Ḥuqúqu'lláh* #39.

166. *See* Bahá'u'lláh, *Ḥuqúqu'lláh* #31; Research Department of the Universal House of Justice, cited in *A Wider Horizon*, p. 171.

167. Research Department of the Universal House of Justice, quoted in *A Wider Horizon*, p. 173.

168. *A Wider Horizon*, p. 91.

169. Research Department of the Universal House of Justice, quoted in *A Wider Horizon*, p. 173.

170. Bahá'u'lláh, *Ḥuqúqu'lláh* #6.

171. Bahá'u'lláh, *Ḥuqúqu'lláh* #7.

172. Bahá'u'lláh, *Ḥuqúqu'lláh* #36.

173. Bahá'u'lláh, *Ḥuqúqu'lláh* #2.

174. *Kitáb-i-Aqdas*, parag. 97.

175. 'Abdu'l-Bahá, *Ḥuqúqu'lláh* #62.

176. Universal House of Justice, *Ḥuqúqu'lláh* #100.

177. *A Wider Horizon*, p. 171.

178. *Wellspring of Guidance*, p. 19.

179. Universal House of Justice, letter dated January 4, 1994, to all National Spiritual Assemblies, quoting Isaiah 2:2.

180. Universal House of Justice, letter dated January 4, 1994, to all National Spiritual Assemblies.

181. *See* Universal House of Justice, letter dated January 4, 1994, to all National Spiritual Assemblies.

182. Universal House of Justice, letter dated Riḍván 151 (1994), to the Bahá'ís of the World.

183. *Kitáb-i-Aqdas*, parag. 74.

184. *See Bahá'í Administration*, p. 186.

185. *Gleanings from the Writings of Bahá'u'lláh*, p. 250.

186. *Selections from the Writings of 'Abdu'l-Bahá*, p. 3.

187. *Kitáb-i-Aqdas*, parag. 33.

188. *Paris Talks*, pp. 176-77.

189. *Wellspring of Guidance*, p. 95.

190. *Gleanings from the Writings of Bahá'u'lláh*, p. 334.

191. 'Abdu'l-Bahá, quoted in *The World Order of Bahá'u'lláh*, p. 133.

192. 'Abdu'l-Bahá, quoted in *The World Order of Bahá'u'lláh*, p. 139.

193. *The Promulgation of Universal Peace*, p. 8.

194. *A Wider Horizon*, p. 66.

195. 'Abdu'l-Bahá, *Stirring of the Spirit* #7.

196. 'Abdu'l-Bahá, *Stirring of the Spirit* #4.

197. *Kitáb-i-Aqdas*, Note #82.

198. 'Abdu'l-Bahá, *Stirring of the Spirit* #17.

199. *Selections from the Writings of 'Abdu'l-Bahá*, p. 91.

200. *Bahá'í Administration*, p. 88.

201. *See* Universal House of Justice, *Consultation* #44.

202. 'Abdu'l-Bahá, *Consultation* #9.

203. *The Promulgation of Universal Peace*, p. 72.

204. 'Abdu'l-Bahá, *Consultation* #10.

205. 'Abdu'l-Bahá, *Consultation* #10.

206. 'Abdu'l-Bahá, *Consultation* #9.

207. 'Abdu'l-Bahá, *Consultation* #12.

208. Bahá'u'lláh, *Consultation* #1.

209. 'Abdu'l-Bahá, *Spiritual Foundations* #27.

210. Shoghi Effendi, *Spiritual Foundations* #42.

211. On behalf of Shoghi Effendi, *Lights of Guidance*, p. 465.

212. On behalf of Shoghi Effendi, *Lights of Guidance*, p. 465.

213. *Kitáb-i-Aqdas*, Questions and Answers #14.

214. Universal House of Justice, *Kitáb-i-Aqdas*, Introduction, p. 1.

215. Universal House of Justice, *Kitáb-i-Aqdas*, Introduction, p. 1.

216. *See God Passes By*, p. 213.

217. *See God Passes By*, pp. 213-14.

218. Universal House of Justice, letter dated March 5, 1993, to the Bahá'ís of the World.

219. *God Passes By*, p. 139.

220. *God Passes By*, p. 140.

221. *God Passes By*, p. 139.

222. On behalf of Shoghi Effendi, *Deepening* #106.

223. On behalf of Shoghi Effendi, *Deepening* #97.

224. *Hidden Words*, preface.

225. *See God Passes By*, p. 140.

226. *God Passes By*, p. 140.

227. 'Abdu'l-Bahá, *Deepening* #39.

228. *God Passes By*, p. 140.

229. *God Passes By*, p. 140.

230. *The Seven Valleys and the Four Valleys*, p. 4.

231. See *God Passes By*, p. 140.

232. *God Passes By*, p. 216.

233. *God Passes By*, p. 216.

234. *Selections from the Writings of 'Abdu'l-Bahá*, p. 79.

235. *God Passes By*, p. 238.

236. *Tablets of Bahá'u'lláh*, p. 221.

237. Universal House of Justice, letter dated January 4, 1994, to all National Spiritual Assemblies.

238. *God Passes By*, p. 219.

239. *God Passes By*, p. 219.

240. Bahá'u'lláh, quoted in *The Promised Day Is Come*, p. 46.

241. 'Abdu'l-Bahá, quoted in *The Promised Day Is Come*, p. 46.

242. *God Passes By*, p. 206.

243. *God Passes By*, p. 212.

244. Shoghi Effendi, quoted in *The Priceless Pearl*, p. 218.

245. On behalf of Shoghi Effendi, *Deepening* #126.

246. On behalf of Shoghi Effendi, *The Individual and Teaching* #46.

247. On behalf of Shoghi Effendi, *Deepening* #149.

248. *God Passes By*, p. 23.

249. *God Passes By*, pp. 24-25.

250. *God Passes By*, p. 26.

251. *God Passes By*, p. 328.

252. *God Passes By*, p. 325.

253. See *God Passes By*, p. 328.

254. *God Passes By*, p. 325.

255. Universal House of Justice, letter dated Ridván 150 (1993), to the Bahá'ís of the World.

256. *Citadel of Faith*, p. 130.

257. *The World Order of Bahá'u'lláh*, p. 87.

258. *God Passes By*, p. 324.

259. Universal House of Justice, letter dated May 19, 1994, to the National Spiritual Assembly of the Bahá'ís of the United States.

260. See Universal House of Justice, letter dated May 19, 1994, to the National Spiritual Assembly of the Bahá'ís of the United States.

261. *God Passes By*, p. 268.

262. See on behalf of Shoghi Effendi, *Lights of Guidance*, p. 439.

263. On behalf of Shoghi Effendi, *Deepening* #106.

264. *The World Order of Bahá'u'lláh*, p. 37.

265. *God Passes By*, p. 242.

266. On behalf of Shoghi Effendi, *Lights of Guidance*, pp. 438-39.

267. *God Passes By*, p. 281.

268. *The World Order of Bahá'u'lláh*, p. 99.

269. On behalf of Shoghi Effendi, *Deepening* #123.

270. *The Priceless Pearl*, p. 213.

271. *The Promised Day Is Come*, p. 116.

272. *See* Universal House of Justice, letter dated May 19, 1994, to the National Spiritual Assembly of the Bahá'ís of the United States.

273. On behalf of Shoghi Effendi, *Deepening* #106.

274. *The World Order of Bahá'u'lláh*, p. 123.

275. *Messages from the Universal House of Justice (1968-1973)*, p. 115.

276. *A Wider Horizon*, p. 58.

277. *The Four Year Plan*, p. 3.

278. *Tablets of Bahá'u'lláh*, p. 200.

279. *Citadel of Faith*, p. 25.

280. Research Department of the Universal House of Justice, quoted in *A Wider Horizon*, p. 173.

281. Because the value of gold fluctuates, the believer must ascertain its value in calculating Ḥuqúqu'lláh.

282. *See Ḥuqúqu'lláh: A Study Guide*, pp. 4-6.

283. On behalf of Shoghi Effendi, quoted in *Wellspring of Guidance*, p. 69.

284. *Prayers and Meditations*, p. 67.

285. *Kitáb-i-Aqdas*, Note #107.

286. *Kitáb-i-Aqdas*, parag. 16.